D1348176

First published in Great Britain in 2017 by
Pen & Sword History
an imprint of
Pen & Sword Books Ltd
47 Church Street
Barnsley
South Yorkshire
S70 2AS

ISBN 978 1 47389 417 4

A CIP catalogue record for this book is
available from the British Library.

Printed and bound in Malta by Gutenberg Press Ltd.

Pen & Sword Books Ltd incorporates the Imprints of Pen & Sword Books
Archaeology, Atlas, Aviation, Battleground, Discovery, Family History, History,
Maritime, Military, Naval, Politics, Railways, Select, Transport, True Crime,
Fiction, Frontline Books, Leo Cooper, Praetorian Press, Seaforth Publishing,
Wharncliffe and White Owl.

For a complete list of Pen & Sword titles please contact
PEN & SWORD BOOKS LIMITED
47 Church Street, Barnsley, South Yorkshire, S70 2AS, England
E-mail: enquiries@pen-and-sword.co.uk
Website: www.pen-and-sword.co.uk

Contents

List of Illustrations

Acknowledgements

I would first and foremost like to thank my lovely wife Holly for her patience and support, along with our four children Sebastian, Anastasia, Alexandre and Callidora. You're the light of my life.

Thank you to Claire Hopkins and everyone at Pen and Sword Books for believing in me and this project. Also a special thanks to Karyn Burnham for her fantastic editorial assistance.

Special thanks also to author MaryJo Ignoffo and finally Phillipp Mimkes of the CBG Network.

Introduction

A brand is often developed around a name, logo, distinct packaging and/or a dedicated mascot. Brand name products are such a part of our daily life and identity that it is difficult to imagine a world where they don't exist. There was a time, not all that long ago, when we weren't defined by the type of car we drove or the brand of clothing or shoes on our bodies. Today, our culture thrives on brands in every facet of our life. These brands have all emerged into the post-Industrial Revolution marketplace and have become an enduring part of our daily lives over the past century. You might think of Bayer when you have a headache, Coca-Cola when you want a drink and perhaps Ford when you're car shopping. These brands are taken for granted today, but they all started somewhere and for many of the brands you know and love, their roots are firmly planted in dark, twisted, and sometimes violent, origins. These aren't the stories that you'll read on the carefully crafted and orchestrated modern corporate histories of companies like Chanel or Adidas. These are the true stories of the brands you know and the often very flawed individuals who created them.

The landscape of both life and industry were very different prior to the events of the Industrial Revolution. The inception of brand names and corporations is relatively new; before the development of mass manufacturing and industrialisation one had to rely on self-production or regionally produced products. Society, in both America and Europe, was comprised primarily of rural and agrarian culture. There were some cities, like London, that had grown and expanded as a capital city, but most of the towns and villages were self-sustaining. If you lived in a village you would have your own on-site bakers, butchers and blacksmiths, and you would often have to hunt for, or grow, most of your own food. If you lived in a rural setting and wanted clothing, food or other goods, there were no stores to visit. If you were lucky you had in-demand goods to barter and trade for other goods or services, but this process was spotty and largely unorganised. The more common occurrence was malnourishment and even starvation when things got difficult. There were no food banks or charities. If there was a bad crop or other pressingly negative issues in your region, any neighbours you had were likely suffering to a similar degree.

This way of living carried over to the Americas in the seventeenth century, when the thirteen colonies that would eventually become the United States were settled. The colonies would self-govern, even though there was still the British monarchy to answer to back at home across the ocean. The local landowners would vote for a provincial government and governor to oversee the goings-on there. When you came to the 'new world' it was, literally, starting over. There were no buildings and no cities or roads. There was only wilderness and the Native Americans who already resided there.

This way of life would soon change, as the Industrial Revolution began to take shape in England. There were certain factors that were necessary for one central area to be the focal point of the coming industrialisation; the demands of the eighteenth and nineteenth century included vital, and bountiful, naturally occurring deposits of commodities like coal and iron ore. Other materials were needed, but if a country had a vast colonisation system in place around the world, then various raw materials could be easily mined and imported. The best option in the world at the time and that was Britain. It was the natural birthplace of big industry. In eighteenth-century Britain, the textile and iron industries were transformed in a major way.

Cottage industry used to be the cornerstone of the textile market. In order to get the best version of 'mass' production in those days the work would be distributed to workers to complete in their homes on their own time. This disorganised and unsupervised way of doing things left the industry plagued with overdue deadlines and inconsistent returns. Still, it was the best and most efficient way of doing things until the age of mechanisation was born. It was in 1764 that weaver and inventor James Hargreaves developed one of the first methods for spinning spools of yarn, called the 'spinning jenny'. This invention was vital in response to the 'flying shuttle', which was introduced by John Kay in 1733. The flying shuttle would allow cloth to be woven on a wider scale. The device could even be attached to a machine and mechanised, a development that was met with much resistance from weavers at the time. The flying shuttle would double the productivity, so the demand for yarn grew. The spinning jenny ('jenny' was slang for engine) would allow the worker to manipulate several spools at once, for a far greater output. There were over 20,000 spinning jenny machines in use around England by the time of Kay's death in 1778. Around the same time, the inventor Samuel Crompton was developing a 'mule-jenny', which was later dubbed the 'spinning mule'. This device built upon the previous inventions and would spin cotton and other fibres into a strong, thin yarn. There were over fifty million mule spindles in use in Lancashire alone! These all led to the invention by Edmund Cartwright of the 'power loom' in the 1780s.

It was Englishman Abraham Darby that would revolutionise the iron industry. The industry had to rely solely on charcoal to run the furnaces necessary to separate the iron from iron ore. The issue with this is that the volume of product that can be produced is completely dependent on the rate of tree growth, as wood is the essential component of charcoal. Rapid deforestation was beginning to catch-up with the industry and it was in need of a new and more sustainable fuel source. Darby developed a system that utilised coke as the primary component. Coke is a fuel source that is made from coal that undergoes a process of synthesis, rather than occurring naturally. In 1709, Darby's coke-fired blast furnace was introduced as a method for casting iron. A key component of the Industrial Revolution was the mass availability and cheaper pricing of iron, both of which were possible thanks largely to Darby's innovation.

The modernisation of the textile and iron industries were major factors in the Industrial Revolution, but it was the inception of the steam engine that would really tip the scales. Englishman Thomas Newcomen was an ironmonger by trade. He introduced the atmospheric engine, the world's first commercial steam engine, in 1712. The engine was first developed to pump the water out of mines, as the flooding of coal and tin mines was a major safety and productivity concern. The steam engine would eventually be adapted to power major machinery, trains and ships. James Watt improved upon the steam engine design with a ten-horsepower continuous rotary engine in 1781.

It was the railways that would push the world forward into mass industrialisation. The first glimpses of a railway network came with the advent of the steam locomotive in 1803. British inventor and mechanical engineer Richard Trevithick was the brilliant mind behind the construction and inception of the world's first railway steam locomotive. The young engineer had a knack for identifying and solving problems that other more educated engineers had difficulty with. Trevithick was a natural in his field and his innovations would change the way we transport both people and goods. Prior to the steam locomotive, the transportation of items utilising horse and carriage, was quite unreliable, vulnerable and slow. Trevithick's engine was half the cost of Watt's model, so it quickly dominated the market, rendering the out-dated Watt type obsolete.

The first transcontinental railroad was constructed in America between 1863 and 1869. The final spike, dubbed the golden spike, was driven into the railroad at Promontory Point, Utah, on 10 May 1869, by Central Pacific Railroad Company head Leland Stanford. The railroad united the country for the first time and made transport safer across the wild plains of the Midwest and created the ability to quickly ship products across the vast divide of the United States in a timely manner.

The Birth of the Brand Name

Brand name products weren't a common sight in the pre-industrialised world, but they did exist. The practice of livestock branding, for example, has been utilised since ancient times. This was more for the practicality of distinguishing your livestock from others rather than any boasting of a particular quality of product. The term brand is derived from the Scandinavian Old Norse language word 'brandr', which means 'burn'. In ancient times the practice was that a creator would burn their symbol or mark into their products, hence the term 'brand'.

The idea of signing or branding your work if you were an artist or a craftsman dates back as early as the first century. A little known glass blower by the name Ennion was not only the first known glass blower in history, but was also the first known brand. Ennion didn't just sign his pieces, he would put an entire message on the bottom. His work would read 'Ennion epoiese', which was Greek for 'Ennion made me'. The idea of a lasting brand would later begin to emerge. The Belgian beer company Stella Artois, for example, has been using a similar logo and their brand name since their inception in 1366. There are a handful of brands that emerged over the centuries, but few that still exist today. The majority of brands that we know today were founded in the nineteenth or twentieth centuries.

When the concept of the mass-manufactured brands emerged during the Industrial Revolution, companies were finally able to transport their products long distances and engage in new markets. The major challenge that came with this development was for people to trust and try-out a non-local product. Prior to this time, most products were locally produced and the consumers often knew the people that made it. The concept of trusting in your local area and the pride that can come with even the smallest village or town is still prevalent today.

The marketplace also changed with the birth of the mail order catalogue. There were times throughout history that catalogues were used, primarily by book publishers to notify buyers of their various titles, but the catalogue industry really boomed in the nineteenth century. The first mail-order catalogue in the United States was sent out by Tiffany in 1845. Montgomery Ward soon followed suit in 1872, and Sears in 1888. The ability to handpick products from watches, clothing and sporting goods to automobiles and even homes became an intoxicating mainstay in American culture. The ability to ship products around the nation made it easy for regional companies to expand. The stores would often become the brand, like in the case of the Sears home. Sears, Roebuck and Company sold upwards of 70,000 of their mail order catalogue homes between 1908 and 1940.

It began with the catalogue, but the expansion of the brand name continued to grow, as the regional product began to dissolve and the national and even international product marketplace emerged. The marketplace was flooded with various products that often made outrageous claims, some that were founded and many that weren't. If your product was reputable it became necessary to distinguish yourself from the herd. A company making a good quality product needed to earn the trust of the regional consumer and they began to build that trust through brand names and advertising. The comfort of knowing that, as a consumer, every time you pick up a Coca-Cola you get the exact same quality of product is what the major corporations of today were built upon. These corporations are often seen now as cold, faceless and inhuman entities, but many of them began as individuals struggling to carve out a place for their product in the competitive marketplace.

In today's world all major corporations have mission statements and 'corporate culture' that help to ensure a certain level of behaviour within the company for all interactions internal and external. There are checks and balances that should ideally keep scandal and disgrace at a minimum and far away from the cherished brand names that are the cornerstone of their business. Historically however, there were no guidelines to keep Bayer away from getting into bed with the Nazis, or to keep Henry Ford from publishing and distributing radical anti-Semitic materials. Corporations like to disavow these dark pasts today, but the study of history demands examination and understanding of truth, even when it becomes inconvenient. This book is intended to enlighten and educate about often hidden parts of brand histories that are often overlooked, and is in no way intended to reflect upon or undermine the far more stable culture that many of these companies and their employees have created today.

In these pages you will read about some disturbing, bizarre and even despicable actions by some of those responsible for the major brand names we know and love today. I want to point out that this in no way reflects on the current companies and corporations that produce these products. These companies were often founded generations ago and those responsible for them are no longer with us. Those that run these companies today are charitable, professional and certainly not associated with any of these controversial beginnings.

Chapter One

Coca-Cola: The Drug-Addled Drink

To many, Coca-Cola is a delicious drink, as American as apple pie. The true origins of this popular soda pop, however, can be a bit murky. Coke is the number one best-selling soft drink in the world and it has a modern day image that projects unity and love to all the world's citizens. It's certainly an interesting thought that without the divisive American Civil War, the world wouldn't have Coca-Cola today, and that its creator wasn't fighting for Abraham Lincoln and the victorious North, but rather for the Confederate South, the side of the conflict that was advocating for the continuation of slavery.

There is a long-standing urban legend that insists Coca-Cola earned its name from the cocaine content in the original soft drink. Coca-Cola publicly disavows any suggestion that their drink ever contained cocaine. In fact, the history that they tell on their official website glazes right over that part of their past without so much as a mention of the controversial topic. The question then begs, did Coca-Cola actually contain cocaine, or is this just a persistent fallacy? What does American alcohol prohibition have to do with the origins of Coca-Cola? Let's explore the long and peculiar history of an American icon.

The Life of John Stith Pemberton

Coca-Cola was created by a man named John Pemberton. John Stith Pemberton was born on 8 July 1831 in Knoxville, Georgia. John and his parents, James and Martha, lived in the city of Rome, Georgia, for the majority of his young life. There is little known about his childhood, but we do know that Pemberton was ambitious as a young man and had a distinct knack towards pharmacology. Pemberton studied medicine, with a focus on pharmacology, at the Reform Medical College of Georgia in Macon. There he became licenced as a 'steam doctor' in the alternative medicine system known as 'Thomsonian medicine' at the age of nineteen. Samuel Thomson invented the Thomsonian system after his wife nearly died when she underwent treatment with conventional medicine. This experience led him to be wary of proper doctors and caused him to use his knowledge of botany to develop a system of herbal remedies that he believed to be superior to the 'poison' that was then modern medicine. A steam doctor relied heavily on herbal treatments and the heat from steam baths to cure patients.

It wouldn't be as a steam doctor that Pemberton would make his mark however, and after twelve years of practice he enlisted in the army of the Confederacy in 1861 and went to war for the values of the South. The American Civil War raged for four bloody years and led to the deaths of nearly one million Americans. The war pivoted on those in the North attempting to block the South from expanding their slavery practices into the western territories of the United States. The South relied upon slave labour to keep their economy stable at the time and didn't take kindly to the idea of being restricted in their growth. The Confederate government was formed and the southern part of the country attempted to secede from the union, desiring to govern itself from that point on. The secession of the South from the union would eventually be quelled by the north, but not before John Pemberton, a Lieutenant Colonel in the army of the Confederacy, was injured severely in the Battle of Columbus.

Pemberton received a deep gash across his chest from a sabre in the battle, a wound that would leave him with considerable pain. The standard painkiller for the era was morphine and that is just what Pemberton got. Pemberton also got what so many others of the era also received: a severe and crippling addiction to morphine. Pemberton fancied himself a man of medicine and vowed to create a miracle drink, one that could rid him and others of their dependency on morphine. The opioid is so powerful that a user can get addicted after only a few doses. It was this chain of events that would lead to the eventual inception of the delicious cola beverage that we all enjoy today.

Pemberton's French Wine Coca

The year was 1886 and the world was rapidly changing amid the Industrial Revolution. In the same year that the giant copper Statue of Liberty was officially dedicated on Liberty Island in New York harbour, and Sir Arthur Conan Doyle wrote the very first Sherlock Holmes mystery, the world's first cola would be invented by an industrious pharmacist from Georgia.

John 'Doc' Pemberton was determined to master the art of invention. He had several failed attempts to produce various hair dyes, pills and elixirs. Success continued to elude him, but he kept forging ahead. During that era, post-civil war rebuilding was sweeping across the region and the idea of a 'new South' was gaining popularity. It was a time when the people of the South were trying to move past the mistakes of the past and cash-in on the industrial and economic boom that was happening in the North. Doc was hoping to get in on the new age of progression.

It was at his drugstore in Columbus, Georgia – Pemberton's Eagle Drug and Chemical House – that he would forge his first success in 1885 with 'Pemberton's French Coca Wine'.

Cocaine was the wonder drug of the nineteenth century. It wasn't uncommon to find products laced with it, as its effects were widely believed to be extremely beneficial. Sigmund Freud was one of the more infamous characters to publicly endorse cocaine therapy as a viable option for patients. Freud considered cocaine to be a fantastic cure for many ailments of the body and mind. Though he would eventually come under fire for his endorsement of the drug when the public backlash against cocaine came about, Freud would never disavow his previous opinions.

Pemberton was inspired by the already popular drink 'Vil Mariani', created by an Angelo Mariani. Mariani, a chemist from Corsica, invented the drink in 1863; it included a mixture of red wine and a rather generous helping of cocaine. Needless to say, the beverage was wildly popular. This was during an era when cocaine was completely legal in Europe and was thought to provide a healthy energy boost. The added benefit of Vin Mariani was that when cocaine and alcohol mix in the human body a third compound is created, called cocaethylene. The effects create a far more euphoric effect than either cocaine or alcohol can provide alone.

Pemberton marketed the drink in much the same way a snake oil salesman would in Victorian times. The ads for the French Wine Coca touted it as: 'The world's great nerve tonic'. The drink claimed itself as a cure for almost anything that could ail you, and was even 'endorsed and recommended by the most eminent medical men'. The drink supposedly cured mental and physical exhaustion, chronic and wasting diseases, dyspepsia, kidney and liver issues, heart disease, melancholia, hysteria, neuralgia, sick headache, throat and lung issues, sleeplessness, despondency and even tired feelings. The drink was said to be 'truly wonderful' and 'strength restoring', and it certainly should have been for the then steep cost of $1.00 per bottle, which would translate to around $20 per bottle in today's market. A bargain price for an elixir that could cure anything and everything.

In reality, Pemberton's French Wine Coca was an alcoholic beverage that was a mixture of kola nut, damiana, coca and of course alcohol. Kola nut has a concentration of caffeine and is actually where the term cola would originate. Damiana is a shrub that is said to help with anxiety, a claim that still hasn't been fully proven. Coca refers to the coca plant, specifically the Erythroxylum coca, which is native to South America. The leaf of the coca plant has a small, naturally occurring amount of cocaine. The levels are so low (.25% to .77% per leaf) that one cannot simply chew, or brew, the leaf to experience the full effects of cocaine. Although drinking brewed leaves may not give one a euphoric high, the leaf of the coca is used for a variety of treatment purposes, including pain relief from broken bones, childbirth, headache, rheumatism and even ulcers. In order to bring the euphoric effects of the coca leaf alkaloids out a chemical extraction process is necessary. Pemberton used this process for the coca leaf to create a coca wine.

The effects of a coca wine are very distinct from that of, say, snorting cocaine. The high is more subtle and lasts longer, without any need for further doses every half hour to forty-five minutes. The side effect of sexual arousal is still present, in fact John Pemberton himself is said to have boasted his wine as 'a most wonderful invigorator of sexual organs'.

The Temperance Movement

Pemberton soon encountered opposition to his alcoholic wonder drink, when the state of Georgia, where he was still based, passed a law that gave the option to vote for prohibition to each county in the state in 1885. The Temperance movement was in full swing in Georgia, where the Woman's Christian Temperance Union (WCTU) had been active since 1880. The WCTU would eventually help lead the charge towards nationwide prohibition in 1920.

The Temperance movement caught on like wildfire and so many counties in Georgia voted themselves 'dry' that Pemberton was all but out of business, before he really had a chance to grow. It was time for him to make the difficult decision to remove the alcoholic content from his drink and develop an alternate solution. Pemberton's French Wine Coca was soon no more.

According to the official Coca-Cola website, Dr Pemberton created a flavoured syrup and took it to his neighbourhood Jacob's Pharmacy to have it mixed with carbonated water The creation of the drink was, according to the corporate statements, a result of 'simple curiosity' on the part of Pemberton. This version of the truth is a rather glossed-over account of the events of 1886. In reality we know that the business of selling his alcohol-cocaine mixture drink had come to a screeching halt with the implementation of local prohibition and it was this and this alone that actually caused Pemberton to seek out his next cocaine-laced drink.

The Origins of Coca-Cola

It's true that the future of Coca-Cola was very closely tied with the moment that Pemberton and Frank Robinson met. Frank M. Robinson was a veteran of the civil war, having served on the side of the Union. These two men, who would have been trying to kill each other years before on opposite sides of the conflict, now joined together to make history. It was Robinson's speciality in advertising and promotion that would give Pemberton's drink the push forward it needed. Doc Pemberton was doing better at creating products, but he had absolutely no idea how to market them well enough to make an impact.

Pemberton had moved to Atlanta to try and cash-in on the growing marketplace there. He wanted to develop a product that would stand apart from all others. It was in the basement of his Atlanta home that he constructed his own laboratory and he went to work. He would constantly send samples of his test products to the local Jacob Pharmacy. Desperate for something to actually sell, he would try out various combinations, until the feedback he got from the consumers showed that he had found a combination that tested well. Pemberton was finally successful in creating something unique. His drink was the first ever cola, not a type or flavour of cola, but the very first one. We can only imagine living in a world without all of the soda pop choices that we enjoy today. Coca-Cola was finally created on 8 May 1886 and to be among the first to taste such a delicious drink must have been amazing.

They finally had the formula for the cola, but the trick now was to actually get it into the hands of the consumer. The product first needed a name and a logo. Frank Robinson came up with the name Coca-Cola and he wrote the logo in a fancy script from his own hand, and history was made. The drink still uses a logo inspired by that original script to this very day. Robinson knew that he needed a great angle to market the drink and it was the very Temperance movement that brought an end to Pemberton's last invention that would create the perfect nesting ground for his newest and most successful one.

The soda fountain was a cheerful and light-hearted place where you could get yourself an ice cream, mineral water or other various beverages and relax with friends. The popularity of the soda fountain would boom in many parts of Georgia once the Temperance movement began. It was no longer acceptable, or legal, to be in a bar or saloon. In fact, they had all been closed in 1885. The soda fountains quickly became a cultural hub and gathering place to meet with friends and discuss current events, politics and culture. There, men and women alike could converge and socialise, creating a vast and concentrated marketplace for an exciting new drink option. It was in the soda fountain that Coca-Cola would find its audience.

On 29 May 1886 the first ever Coca-Cola advert would appear in print, in the pages of the *Atlanta Constitution* newspaper. The advert, which was largely obscured by other adverts for a hat maker and photographer, read: 'Coca-Cola, Delicious! Refreshing! Exhilarating! Invigorating! The new and popular soda fountain drink, containing the properties of the wonderful Coca plant and the famous Cola nuts.' In the first year of business Pemberton would incur a total cost of $76 in expenses to produce and market Coca-Cola. This would involve sale of twenty-five gallons of syrup, making him $50 in profit. It is not difficult to see that these numbers don't exactly equal success. In debt the first year of business, Pemberton would soon fall ill and become bedridden. It was during this time that Coca-Cola nearly fell to the wayside completely. Pemberton was still addicted to morphine, which wasn't an inexpensive habit. He began to sell off the rights to his formula, eventually selling the patent to Asa Candler in 1888. Pemberton would succumb to stomach cancer on 16 August 1888 at the age of 57. He was buried back in his hometown of Columbus, Georgia, his tombstone emblazoned with the Confederate flag. Pemberton struggled with success and the distraction of his addiction may have played a large part of his constant undoing. Doc Pemberton would not live long enough to grasp what a success his invention would become, but the question must also be pondered, would it have been such a success had he lived and retained control of it?

After purchasing the patent for Coca-Cola in 1888, Asa Candler was responsible for the next stage of the drink's success. In fact, some would say that Candler rescued the drink from certain failure. Candler had gone to Pemberton years before as a young man looking for work, only to be turned away. Proving himself to be a savvy businessman, Candler eventually found success as a druggist, opening his own very successful drugstore. When he was approached to purchase Coca-Cola, Candler originally baulked at the idea, because his drugstore didn't contain a soda fountain in which to sell the drink. It wasn't until Candler actually sampled the drink that he was completely sold on the idea. It could be referred to as the single most important serving of Coke. He was convinced that Coca-Cola could be a national drink with the right marketing, and boy was he right. He believed in Coca-Cola so much that he bought up all rights to distribute the drink. This move towards sole ownership would cost him around $2,300. Candler believed in the potential of Coca-Cola, and thus his aggressive marketing of the product began.

Coca-Cola wasn't the only product that Candler owned. He would simultaneously promote Coke next to one of his other products, De-Lec-Ta-Lave dentifrice, a teeth cleansing powder. Obviously, Coca-Cola would end up being the more successful of the two. Candler was of the belief that just one glass of Coca-Cola would sell any potential customer, so he set out to convince America that his drink was special and not to be missed. The early promotional efforts were made by way of travelling salesmen. They had special card coupons that they would hand out that read: 'This card entitles you to one glass of Coca-Cola at the fountain of any dispenser of genuine Coca-Cola.' There were also flyer hand-outs with detachable cards that were also distributed. It seems like a given that handing out coupons for free samples of product is a great marketing ploy, but at the time when Candler did this, he was a pioneer. Other adverts would try to draw in ladies by mimicking a prescription slip that read: 'Coca-Cola: Revives and Sustains. Take one glass of Coca-Cola when weary with shopping. It imparts energy and vigor.' The idea that cola relieves fatigue and revives the weary was an angle that Candler would play upon for years. The free coupon promotion was a success with $7,700 worth of coupons redeemed in 1895 alone. That equates to 154,000 glasses of Coca-Cola. The sales were beginning to take off, but Candler needed to continue to be industrious with his marketing tactics – after all, you need paying customers too.

Candler would innovate another type of marketing that we still see in today's world. He incorporated the Coca-Cola company logo into all kinds of everyday products, like posters, calendars, notebooks, bookmarks, etc. The idea was to get the product name in front of the customer at every point of their day. It was a wildly successful venture, creating a wide range of products that remain collectible to this day. Coca-Cola was quickly becoming a national drink and securing its spot in the marketplace.

Coca-Cola and Cocaine

Coca-Cola was born during an era when Victorian medicines often included sketchy ingredients and boasted themselves as a remedy for everything from the practical to the absurd. Coca-Cola was no different, in fact the soft drink was originally marketed as an 'Intellectual Beverage' and was again presented as a 'valuable tonic' and 'nerve stimulant', just as Pemberton's French Wine Coca had been.

In time, the public began to turn on products that included coca leaves, due to a perception of increasing amounts of cocaine addiction in the populace. In 1891 a 'thoughtful citizen' wrote into *The Constitution*, an Atlanta newspaper:

> *The drug stores and soda founts are selling enormous quantities of something they call coca cola. It is said to relieve nervousness, and 'that tired feeling' and all that sort of thing, and people are drinking it a dozen times a day. I am told by a physician that the ingredient which makes coca cola so popular is cocaine. There is evidently enough of it in the drink to affect people and it is insidiously but surely getting thousands of people into the cocaine habit, which is ten times worse than alcoholism and as bad as the morphine habit. It is an awful drug and the victims of it are slaves. I have seen it!*

This was a post-industrial revolution era that was still bringing about major innovations and changes in the way that products were thought of from a manufacturing standpoint, and Coca-Cola would soon become available, not just at pharmacies and soda fountains in Georgia, but all across the United States. In 1899 the company began to move away from the soda fountain market and sell mass-market bottles of their product. This move made the drink accessible to people of colour for the very first time. The soda fountains of old were segregated areas, like so many businesses of the era.

The intention wasn't to market to people of all races, but rather just to expand the national scope of the business. The backlash was unexpected, but severe, as reports of 'negro cocaine fiends' were being spread by newspapers nationwide. An editorial in the *Journal of the American Medical Association* even went so far as to say: 'The negroes in some parts of the South are reported as being addicted to a new form of vice – that of 'cocaine sniffing' or the 'coke habit', as it appears to have this name also.' The article goes on to discuss 'the negroes of Kentucky' and the hopes that the cocaine habits there will remain isolated to those areas. There is also talk of how some areas had made it illegal for a doctor to prescribe cocaine to a patient for anything but medicinal purposes.

The major backlash against cocaine was absolutely racially charged, and as evidence anti-narcotic legislation, like the Harrison Narcotics Tax Act was introduced. It would be this purely racist movement against cocaine in the United States that would eventually lead to Coca-Cola removing all traces of the drug from their drink.

In 1908 Dr Hamilton Wright became America's first Opium Commissioner. He attended the Shanghai International Opium Commission in February of 1909 and gave a full report on the subject, which included not only findings on chronic opium use in the United States, but also highlighted what he felt was a problem with cocaine. 'It is certain, however, that the use of cocaine among the lower order of working negroes is quite common.' Wright goes on to say:

> *This class of negro is not willing, as a rule, to go to much trouble or send to any distance for anything, and, for this reason, where he is known to have become debauched by cocaine, it is certain that the drug has been brought directly to him from New York and other Northern States where it is manufactured.*

The Harrison Narcotics Act was: *An Act To provide for the registration of, with collectors of internal revenue, and to impose a special tax on all persons who produce, import, manufacture, compound, deal in, dispense, sell, distribute, or give away opium or coca leaves, their salts, derivatives, or preparations, and for other purposes.* The term narcotic was utilised, so that the act could cover not just opium, but the growing concern regarding cocaine. This law also made allowances for doctors to continue prescribing said narcotics to their patients as a part of normal treatments, but could not supply it to existing addicts to quench their habit.

Coca-Cola began bending to the public pressure and in the early twentieth century began developing processes for lessening the amount of cocaine in the drink and ceased advertising its benefits and use. In 1922, the Jones–Miller Act was passed, which banned the importation of cocaine to the United States. It was discovered years ago that Coca-Cola received a special exception from this law by the government and continued to import the plant. It wasn't until 1929 that the company was able to begin removing the cocaine content completely from their drink, but to this day they still import the narcotic-laced plant.

The coca leaf was still a part of the Coca-Cola mixture in recent years. There was a special extraction process that was developed in conjunction with the government of Peru in the 1980s. This was amidst the Reagan administration's 'war on drugs' campaign, but special permission was given for coca leaves to be imported into the United States to the Stephan Maywood plant. There, the company would have the cocaine removed from the plant through a special process. The cocaine by-product is then sold to Mallinckrodt, a company that purifies the drug into cocaine hydrochloride U.S.P., which is used as a local anaesthetic by many ear, nose and throat doctors. The coca leaves, minus cocaine content, are then sent to Coca-Cola for inclusion in their drink.

Coca-Cola Today

The Coca-Cola company is a corporate giant in today's world. The total assets of Coca-Cola were over ninety billion dollars in 2015. The company is still based in Atlanta, Georgia, but they have grown far past the days of their morally ambiguous Southern Confederate creator and the days of cocaine inclusion. Now, Coca-Cola makes it a point to take a stand in matters of social justice. In a press release in April of 2016 titled: 'The Coca-Cola Company Statement on Importance of Equal Rights for LGBT Community', the company stated their dedication to equal rights for all:

> *The Coca-Cola Company does not support legislation that discriminates. We believe policies that discriminate are contrary to our Company's core values and also negatively affect the lives of our associates, consumers, customers, suppliers, and partners.*

In March 2015 they also expressed publicly their support of marriage equality:

> *As a believer in an inclusive world, The Coca-Cola Company values and celebrates diversity. We have long been a strong supporter of the LGBT community and have advocated for inclusion, equality and diversity through both our policies and practices.*

Coca-Cola totals a staggering 700,000 employees worldwide. They sell 1.9 billion servings of Coke every day and their dividends have steadily increased each year for over fifty years. Coca-Cola merchandise remains collectible, especially the vintage merchandise and advertising materials. Thankfully, Coke is here to stay.

Chapter Two

Hugo Boss: Nazi Fashion

There were many manufacturers involved in the uniforming and arming of the German Nazi soldiers throughout the Second World War, but only one of those companies would become a household name in fashion that remains in the public eye today, and that is Hugo F. Boss. The Hugo Boss company features a namesake that is shrouded in disgrace and subversion, with accusations of forced labour and an allegiance to the National Socialist Party by Boss himself. There is no doubt that Hugo F. Boss agreed with and supported the ideals of the Nazi party, and his clothing company would be one of many that ended up making uniforms for the Nazi troops and the Gestapo prior to and throughout the Second World War.

Hugo Boss Early Life

Hugo Ferdinand Boss was born on 8 July 1885 in the Swabian town of Metzingen, in the Kingdom of Wurttemberg, Germany. Boss was the youngest of four siblings. His parents, Heinrich and Luise Boss, ran a modest lingerie shop, which Boss would eventually inherit when he married Anna Katharin Freysinger in 1908. It would be abnormal for the youngest child to inherit the family business under normal circumstances, but only Hugo and his sister survived infancy, therefore the then traditional responsibility was bestowed upon Hugo. The couple would have one daughter before Hugo enlisted in the German Army in 1914, at the start of the First World War. Hugo never received any medals or promotions while serving in the army, clearly not ambitious about an on-going military career. This isn't surprising for someone who had a family business to fall back on.

The Beginnings of a Business

In 1924, a decade after enlisting in the military, Hugo F. Boss opened his very first clothing factory in his hometown of Metzingen. The start-up required financial support from two local manufacturers, but soon the company was employing twenty to thirty seamstresses. The connection with the Nazis began early, when one of the first major commissions in his first year of business included the now notorious brown shirts for the National Socialist Party.

The ripple effect caused by 'Black Tuesday' in America would change the course of the story of Hugo F. Boss, leading him right into the centre of the Nazis. The stock market on Wall Street crashed on 24 October 1929, driving the United States into the Great Depression, causing rampant unemployment and shattering America's economy. The effect of this crash was also felt around the world and in Germany unemployment began to rise as the economy continued to suffer. The textile manufacturers were hit hard and by 1931 Hugo Boss was facing certain bankruptcy. Boss would make a deal with his creditors that allowed him to continue production, but clearly things weren't going in a good direction for Germany and something needed to be done. This series of events led Hugo F. Boss right to the door of the National Socialist Party, of which he became a literal card-carrying member in 1931, two years before Adolf Hitler would seize power of Germany. The party was promising economic solutions for Germany, including ways to help the unemployment levels that were plaguing the country.

The Third Reich gave a good amount of business to Boss once he became an official party member. This came with restrictions, of course, because what they primarily wanted producing were uniforms and work clothing, but despite this, sales began to grow steadily from 1933 to 1938. Then, in 1938, the big commissions for Nazi uniforms began to flood in. Boss and his workers were thrilled with the influx, feeling that they had finally 'made it'. Boss would peak in profits around 1942, but that is where it would level out, because the Third Reich put a cap on the costs that manufacturers could charge, in an effort to manage their own finances. The Boss factory was a 'Price Category 1', which essentially meant that they had the ability to produce the uniforms that the Nazis needed at the lowest prices possible. Not great news for Hugo Boss, and his company wouldn't develop into a huge corporation until long after his own death.

Prior to the war, Boss had produced everything from the early brown shirts, to black uniforms for the SS, and the Hitler Youth uniforms. During the war the Boss factory produced uniforms primarily for the German armed forces and Waffen-SS. The examination of the Hugo Boss company's role in producing Nazi uniforms may be highlighted in this book, but they were far from the only manufacturer contributing to the cause; Boss was in no way a stand out in terms of production quantities or contributions. They were simply one of many in a vast country working as cogs in the Nazi machine. The fact that Hugo Boss is still a household name in high fashion today, despite the dark beginnings, is what makes it of such interest. It should be noted that while they produced uniforms for the Nazis, there is no reason to assume that Hugo Boss had anything to do with the design of any uniforms.

Forced Labour

The textile manufacturing trade in Nazi Germany wasn't exactly the highest paid job that a worker could have. The uniforms were certainly a necessary part of the German war machine, but the serious workforce moved towards more lucrative trades, mostly involving weaponry and engineering. There was, therefore, a distinct lack of available and skilled workers for the textile industry. Enter one of the darker parts of the affiliation of Hugo F. Boss with the Nazis – forced labour. The Hugo Boss company first employed forced labour in April of 1940. The entire town of Metzingen would come to house a whopping 1,241 forced labourers during the war. There was a point when up to 180 of those workers were being made to work for Hugo Boss. This consisted of 140 forced labourers and forty French prisoners of war.

The majority of the forced workers were transplanted from Bielsko in Poland, because there was already a large textile manufacturing industry there, so the skilled workforce was already trained and ready to go. The Nazi Gestapo brought the workers in to be divided amongst the various textile manufacturers throughout Metzingen. When the workers arrived in Metzingen they were split up by gender; the women were placed with local families, while the men were moved into sheds in a dedicated Hugo Boss company encampment. Investigations into the male workers' camp found that it was at least hygienic, but in 1943 a new camp was built to house all of the workers from the various Metzingen factories. The conditions at this camp were unstable at best, with food sometimes being scarce and the hygiene not to the standards of the previous accommodations. There is some evidence to suggest that Hugo F. Boss took certain measures to help the labourers receive treatment that was at least moderate, providing midday meals to them in the company canteen and trying to keep the female workers out of the camps. These measures were certainly a step in the right direction, but when you're dealing with the topic of slavery, it's all details.

Post-War Fallout

The allied forces occupying Germany at the end of the Second World War finally reached the streets of Metzigen in April of 1945. Between them, the allied forces of America, Britain, France and the Soviets split Germany into occupation zones. The zone that encompassed Metzigen would come to be occupied by the French troops. It was then that the denazification of the region began.

The concept of denazification was an effort to examine all of the public offices and positions of power and control within Nazi Germany and remove all traces of the National Socialist Party from those arenas. The denazification process would come to be especially critical of Hugo F. Boss. The Potsdam Declaration would detail the intentions of the Allied Forces clearly:

All members of the Nazi party who have been more than nominal participants in its activities and all other persons hostile to Allied purposes shall be removed from public and semi-public office and from positions of responsibility in important private undertakings. Such persons shall be replaced by persons who, by their political and moral qualities, are deemed capable of assisting in developing genuine democratic institutions in Germany.

This process would also trickle down to the educational and judicial systems, as well:

German education shall be so controlled as completely to eliminate Nazi and militarist doctrines and to make possible the successful development of democratic ideas. The judicial system will be reorganized in accordance with the principles of democracy, of justice under law, and of equal rights for all citizens without distinction of race, nationality or religion. The administration of affairs in Germany should be directed toward the decentralization of the political structure and the development of local responsibility. To this end: Local self-government shall be restored throughout Germany on democratic principles and in particular through elective councils as rapidly as is consistent with military security and the purposes of military occupation; All democratic political parties with rights of assembly and of public discussions shall be allowed and encouraged throughout Germany

The denazification process wasn't intended primarily to remove or examine business owners, but rather was meant to focus on political offices. The unique amount of involvement with the National Socialist

Party that Boss enjoyed made him a prime candidate to be singled out. Hugo F. Boss was not only an active member of the Nazi party himself, but he had also become good friends with the despised regional Nazi leader, Georg Rath. The council decided to fine Boss a hefty 100,000 reichmarks, the second highest fine imposed in the region. It is clear that the French felt that Boss needed to be made an example of. Ultimately, Hugo F. Boss was classified by the French as a 'follower', thus he only received the punishment of a fine.

Hugo F. Boss would die of a tooth abscess in his lifelong home of Metzingen on 9 August 1948, at the age of 63.

The Hugo Boss Company Apologises

The dark past of Hugo F. Boss plagued the fashion company that still brandishes his tainted name for years so, in an effort to expose the whole truth, the Hugo Boss company commissioned a historical study. The self-commissioned study was extremely revealing. It was made public by the Hugo Boss company in August 2011.

The company issued the following statement on their official website:

> *The study and its summary were produced in cooperation with the highly respected Gesellschaft für Unternehmensgeschichte – a German institution devoted to chronicling corporate histories – and its independent historians. The Group wishes to emphasize that it was not involved in the research or writing and that no influence whatsoever was brought to bear concerning the study's form or content.*
>
> *In the past HUGO BOSS AG has often been confronted by vague statements regarding its history. Hugo Ferdinand Boss established his workshop in 1924, as a consequence of which his company operated during the Third Reich and the Second World War. During this period the factory employed 140 forced labourers (the majority of them women) and 40 French prisoners of war. When the Group became aware of this fact, it made a contribution to the international fund set up to compensate former forced labourers.*
>
> *Out of respect to everyone involved, the Group has published this new study with the aim of adding clarity and objectivity to the discussion. It also wishes to express its profound regret to those who suffered harm or hardship at the factory run by Hugo Ferdinand Boss under National Socialist rule.*

Continuing Controversy

The Hugo Boss controversy continues to come to light from time to time. In fact, just a few years ago, shock-comedian Russell Brand was holding the microphone at the *GQ* Fashion Awards to accept the Oracle Award. The annual event, which was sponsored by the Hugo Boss company, included an audience of designers and celebrities. Following British Conservative politician Boris Johnson, a somewhat out-of-place character at the fashion awards, Brand made light of the historical origins that Hugo Boss shares with the Nazis:

> *Glad to grace the stage where Boris Johnson has just made light of the use of chemical weapons in Syria. Meaning that GQ can now stand for 'Genocide Quips'. I mention that only to make the next comment a bit lighter, because if any of you know a little bit about history and fashion, you'll know Hugo Boss made the uniforms for the Nazis. The Nazis did have flaws, but you know they did look fucking fantastic, lets face it. While they were killing people on the basis of their religion and sexuality. Genocide Quips are okay, no its okay its okay its already been sanctioned…its all cool.*

One might assume that the countless headlines in newspapers and online after the event would highlight the lesser-known public fact that Hugo F. Boss was a member of the Nazi party, but instead there was a collective outrage over the nerve of Russell Brand for bringing up the tender subject of the company's sketchy history: 'Why Russell Brand's Nazi barbs didn't go over well with Hugo Boss', 'Why Russell Brand Made A Controversial Nazi Joke About Hugo Boss', 'Russell Brand stuns GQ Men Of The Year audience with Nazi rant and salute' and 'Russell Brand "thrown out of *GQ* after-party" for offensive Nazi jibes about event sponsors Hugo Boss'.

Apparently the joke was so poorly received by the sponsors of the event that *GQ* editor Dylan Jones personally kicked Brand out of the after-show party. This isn't terribly surprising, considering that the Hugo Boss company had donated a whopping £250,000 to throw the event. Russell Brand later posted the following recount of the event on his official Twitter account: *GQ editor: 'What you did was very offensive to Hugo Boss.' Me: 'What Hugo Boss did was very offensive to the Jews.'* #GQAwards #nazitailor

GQ Magazine wasn't done with punishing Brand. They went on to erase all mention of him in their 'Men of the Year' issue, where Brand had been planned as a focal point. In expected fashion, Russell Brand tweeted the following in retort:

'GQ cleansed me from their issue. That's what they do when they don't like something. I guess that's why they dig the Nazis'.

Chapter Three

Henry Ford: The Jewish Conspiracy

There are several well-known car brands in our world today, but probably none that have the historical significance and reputation of the Ford Motor Company. Founder Henry Ford rose from an engineer to the sole manufacturer of the first mass-produced and affordable automobile. Today, the Ford brand lives on as an icon in the industry, but there was more than one side to the engineering genius that was Henry Ford. He held some very positive social views, that the common people should be able to afford their own automobile for example, and in many ways he was a generous family man and philanthropist. Unfortunately, he was also rabidly anti-Semitic, convinced that there was an international Jewish conspiracy that had the aim of taking down America. Ford's views would become so radical and so highly circulated that they would even find their way as far as Hitler and his vicious Nazi Party in pre-Second World War Germany. Henry Ford is one of a handful of people from the past century who changed the world. The delicate balance of greatness and madness continue to define Ford's legacy to this day.

The History of the Automobile

Since the days of prehistory, the primary modes of transportation had been some combination of horses pulling a carriage. The roots of this transport can be traced back to the Celts and the ancient Mesopotamians. It wasn't until the industrial revolution that the tide began to finally turn. The end of the nineteenth century saw human inspiration at an all-time high and various kinds of motorised transportation began to emerge. The true automobile surge came in America after the turn of the twentieth century, when Henry Ford began to revolutionise the means and standards of production in his factories. This may be an important point in history, but it is also important to understand the long journey that the automobile took to get there, in order to appreciate the full impact that Ford made, not only on the marketplace, but on society itself.

The world has always been vast and wild and the question of how to best travel efficiently from one area to another has often been the subject of thought and innovation. Humans have been utilising horse and carriage combinations for thousands of years.

The use of horses was still the most efficient answer to the concern of travel, both local and long distances, until the eighteenth century. The old ways of travel may have sustained the world at the time, but using a horse-drawn carriage brought its own difficulties. A horse requires rest, food, water, husbandry, and care; to properly maintain a horse can be both expensive and time consuming. Naturally, when a more efficient mode of transportation was on the horizon, the days of the horse and buggy were numbered.

One of the early pioneers of the automobile industry hailed from Paris, France, in the commune Boulogne-Billancourt in the western suburbs. Louie Renault spent long hours working in his father's tool shed, until one fateful Christmas Eve in 1898. That day, Louis Renault finished his automobile. He had saved money from his time in the military, so that he could purchase a De-Dion three-wheeler and modified it into a four-wheeler. The De-Dion was a motor-powered tricycle, but the addition of the fourth wheel drastically changed the landscape of motorised vehicles. The Renault was able to climb hills easily and could speed along efficiently, with no clanking belts or chains. Louie drove it to a Christmas party in order to show it off. The partygoers were quite impressed and they ordered a whopping twenty-four cars on the spot.

Louis was ready to go into business for himself. With his brothers, he established the Renault Frères Company and they manufactured automobiles on their family land in Billancourt. The older brothers handled the business side of things, while Louie dedicated his time to the design and manufacturing angle of the company. Sixty of the Renault vehicles were sold over six months. To purchase a Renault cost well over $1,000 (approximately $27,000 in 2016 or £21,500, which made it rather expensive for the average consumer of the era. The brothers were smart with their profits and re-invested their money into the business. Within a few years, they managed to double the size of the business and employ over one hundred people. Louis was a demanding perfectionist, but he expected excellence from himself as well as his employees. The Renaults were able to obtain various achievements in auto racing, which had become a popular attraction at the turn of the century amongst the well-off Parisians.

In the 1901 Paris-Bordeaux-Paris car race the Renaults won the first four places. In the Paris-Berlin race, the first three places, and in 1902 Marcel Renault won against Mercedes and Panhard. The many achievements gained by the Renaults provided their vehicles with a good amount of prestige and popularity throughout France. In 1903, tragedy struck when Marcel Renault was killed after losing control of his race car, but the company continued to move forward despite the loss of one brother, with Louis taking on more responsibilities. Louis continued to develop new ideas and one of those was to adapt their automobile to better fit the lives of the consumer.

In 1904 they released a roomier vehicle that comfortably seated four passengers. It was a move that would pave the way to the future of the company, for it was the following year that their business model would suddenly change. A Paris taxi company put in an order to Renault for a whopping 250 automobiles. Three years later the company had sold over 1,000 taxis around Europe. Renault soon became the largest auto producer in France, selling over 3,000 vehicles. Louis began to create models for specific sections of society, everything from an economy two cylinder, two-seater car, to a Coupe de Ville and a limousine for luxury.

In 1886 German Karl Benz introduced his Benz Patent-Motorwagen, which is often regarded as the first modern automobile, but it would be Gottlieb that first brought his design to America. In 1888 Gottlieb Daimler and Steinway & Sons came to a distribution agreement that would bring Daimler vehicles to the United States of America. The first American-made car was the Duryea automobile, built by the Duryea Motor Wagon Company in 1893. The open-air car featured a gasoline-powered one-cylinder engine.

Ransom Olds was also experimenting during the time that Henry Ford was beginning to work with motor carriages. A fire destroyed the Olds factory in 1901 and only a curved-dash model vehicle survived. Olds used the remaining car as a prototype and through some strategic subcontracting he managed to produce over 400 cars that year. The Oldsmobile was designed for a larger consumer base, not just the wealthy. It was extremely economical and sturdy.

Henry Ford entered the marketplace with his vehicles in 1908, but automakers quickly encountered an issue, thanks to the Seldin patent. George B. Seldin was a patent attorney that had the ingenious idea of getting a patent on all gasoline-powered vehicles, so it become impossible for anyone to produce a gas-powered vehicle without paying a healthy royalty to Seldin. This hiccup was nothing more than an annoyance and didn't stop the industry from experiencing plenty of growth. Henry Ford would challenge the Seldin monopoly in court and in 1911 he won his final victory over it, freeing all automakers from the confines of Seldin's patent.

The automobile began to change from a novelty item for the wealthy into a viable transportation option for the ordinary citizen, thanks to the efforts of Henry Ford. Slowly, but surely the streets were becoming filled with noisy cars rather than horse drawn carriages. There was a new enthusiasm in developing motorised vehicles as a means of transport for all. There were more than eight million cars on the road by 1926, and by 1929 forty-five million Americans were using cars as a means to vacation across the country. The number of service stations would increase tenfold throughout the 1920s, along with roadside restaurants and motels. Los Angeles, California, was the first major city to be built around the use of the car and helped to develop a 'car culture' that would spread across the nation.

During the Great Depression of the 1930s, the car allowed families to escape the dustbowl by heading out West in search of a new life. The car was such an important part of American life that by the 1930s, citizens owned more cars than either telephones or bathtubs. The roads began to get paved and citizens were put to work, building bridges and tunnels to accommodate the intense growth of traffic on the roads. The 1939 World's Fair was centred largely around the automobile industry, with several major companies showing off their new innovations and advances. The start of the Second World War halted the progress of the car for a time, but not before Henry Ford revolutionised the industry.

Henry Ford's Early Life and Career

Henry Ford was born on 30 July 1863, in Greenfield Township, Michigan. The son of farmers, he never completed the eighth grade, but from a young age Henry showed a serious interest in the then modern study of mechanics. His parents supported his ambitions by constructing a workbench for him in the already cramped kitchen. Henry spent a lot of time at his workbench, tinkering and teaching himself all about how things worked. Life on the farm was very isolating to Ford and this gave him a great perspective later in life on the need for affordable transportation for the common person and how the new idea of a horseless carriage could transform the world.

Ford worked as a machinist throughout his twenties, until he got the opportunity to work for Thomas Edison. Henry Ford began his career as an engineer for the Edison Illuminating Company in 1891, where he rose to the rank of Chief Engineer in 1893. It was during this time that Ford would experiment with gasoline engines and self-propelled horseless carriages, such as his quadricycle. Ford eventually crossed paths with Edison himself in 1896 and was given encouragement to move forward with a second vehicle. Ford launched his quadricycle and tested it around Detroit on 4 June, 1896.

The horseless carriage featured 28in bicycle wheels, no brakes, and could reach top speeds of up to 20mph. The quadricycle wasn't quite the vehicle Ford envisioned and had a few major flaws, such as the inability to go in reverse and a propensity to overheat.

Ford decided that it was time to branch out on his own and on 5 August, 1899, he founded the Detroit Automobile Company. He began to produce automobiles, backed by Detroit lumber baron William H. Murphy. America had the railroads, but other transportation methods were terribly inconvenient. During this time an automobile-manufacturing boom hit the city and over fifty more companies sprung up that same year, with more to follow the next year. The majority of these companies would inevitably fail. The Detroit Automobile Company produced cars for two years, but was ultimately unsuccessful. Ford attributed this to a poor quality product that was overpriced. Henry Ford was beginning to form a vision for the automobile industry and it required him to have more control over all aspects of production.

The next venture that Ford undertook was far more successful, but in order to attract backers he had to do something bold. Ford built a race car in secret to help build publicity for himself. On 10 October 1901, Ford took on famous racing driver Alexander Winston in a one-on-one sweepstakes race. Ford had no money or reputation to hire a real driver, so he put himself behind the wheel. It was a risky venture, to be sure, but Henry Ford was never afraid to take the risks necessary to succeed. He also didn't fear the potential failure; in fact it seemed to drive him on. On the sixth lap, Ford closed the gap and his rival's engine overheated; Ford won by nearly a mile. It was as a result of this spectacle that Ford was able to forge the Ford Motor Company.

The journey started with Ford & Malcomson Ltd., which was a partnership he formed with coal dealer Alexander Y. Malcomson. The two leased a factory and made a deal with the Dodge Brothers, John and Horace, and Ford began work on designing his inexpensive automobile. After some shifting around of investors, the company would be rebranded on 16 June 1903 as the Ford Motor Company. Ford managed to get the then famous racing driver, Barney Oldfield, to drive his Ford 999 model across the country, which is what it took to get a brand recognised at the turn of the twentieth century. Ford would also find good promotion in backing the early days of the Indianapolis 500 race in the coming years. The Ford Model N was introduced to the marketplace and sold for two years from 1906 for a price of $600 ($15,127.50 in today's terms). The relative success of this car emboldened Ford and he went back to work, developing an even better model for the masses.

Henry Ford was driven, and sure of his own vision, but not everyone felt the same way. He duped backers by producing parts for cars he never intended to build. Ford used their money and time instead to work on perfecting his magnum opus, the Model T. He had no time for investors or their ideas, in fact he blamed the investors for the past issues he had had. Ford harboured a hatred for the rich and for his own investors.

In 1907 Henry Ford walled off a corner of his factory, wide enough only for the chassis of a car. There was one door that remained locked at all times. Ford put his engineers and team in the secret room to have them develop a new suspension system and engine. Ford himself wasn't shy about getting his hands dirty and worked side by side with his men. His passion and drive took centre stage, far above any position or prestige that he held at the time. It wasn't until later in life that his ego would inflate to a dangerous level.

Ford kept introducing new car models into the marketplace. The Model K was too heavy and expensive, the Model N was lighter, but had an engine in four pieces instead of one block. He kept working his way through the automobile alphabet, working towards the T, where he would finally realise his vision for the people's automobile, something that would connect the country and close the gaps in society.

In October of 1908, after two years of intense development, the Ford Model T would emerge. The car featured new innovations such as a four-cylinder twenty horsepower engine, a much-improved transmission, and a magnetic generator that powered the ignition and lights. The Model T also featured an open top design at first, with an optional add-on cover. The original colour scheme of the car was green, but that would soon change to only black. The Model T weighed 1,200lbs and could reach speeds of up to 40mph. The old horse-drawn carriages could take up to ten hours or more to travel forty miles, so the mobility that the Model T offered was vastly improved. Wells Fargo and Company was one of the more well known stagecoach companies that would transport people across the often dangerous territories, but even those could only travel an average of 5mph with teams of four to six horses. The official Wells Fargo website also adds that the drivers had to stop every twelve miles to change out the horses and every forty-five miles to allow the drivers and passengers to eat.

It was with the introduction of the Model T in 1908 that Ford began to really solidify his position in the marketplace and in the history of the automobile in America. The Model T featured the very first left-side steering wheel, among other innovations that made it the first mass-purchased automobile. The Model T helped to revolutionise the marketplace, primarily because it was so easy to drive and to repair. The four-cylinder vehicle would cost the consumer a whopping $825, which would presently translate to $20,392 (or £14,128) in today's market. This was the first time that a mass market of consumers in America could actually afford their own automobile. Prior to that it was a privilege frill of the wealthy citizens, with the average cost of a vehicle running around $2,000, which is $53,225.79 (£42,189.75) in today's money. The average annual salary in the United States at the time was only around $450, or about $10,000 (£7,900) today, so the price of a car made all the difference. 'I'm going to democratise the automobile,' Ford is said to have declared in 1909. 'When I'm through, everybody will be able to afford one, and about everybody will have one.' It was thanks to this great attitude towards the public that so many could finally realise their dreams of mobility. The Ford Model T gave the citizens the ability to travel outside of their own towns and opened up the country in a way that it hadn't been previously. The added control it gave people over their lives and locations made a huge impact, but if automobiles were going to become the norm, they would need to keep dropping in price to meet the needs of the consumer. Not only did the price start low, but Ford kept dropping it year after year, bringing the cost of the basic touring car down to only $360, or $8,572 (£5,939) today. The sales rose to 472,000 units by 1914, making the Model T so prolific that most Americans of the era actually learned to drive in it.

The Model T, Assembly Line and Ford Workers

The Ford Model T would remain the industry giant with a total number of over 15 million cars produced by the time it was discontinued in 1927, to be replaced by the Model A. The burgeoning film industry would adopt the car as a comedic device, often using the Ford Model T in their chase scenes. The inclusion of the vehicle in the movies would help to put the car in front of a large number of Americans and would help to solidify it as a staple in the marketplace. The Model T held the record for the most produced car until it was dethroned in 1972 by the Volkswagen Beetle. The irony that the Beetle was Adolf Hitler's version of an accessible car that the German people could afford is one that will be clear by the end of this chapter.

Among the innovations that Henry Ford was responsible for, the modern assembly line and the way that his workers were treated were the most notable. Henry Ford is often credited with the invention of the assembly line concept, but that couldn't be further from the truth. In fact, assembly lines have been used throughout history, as seen in the fourteenth century Venetian shipbuilding complex. The Venetian production system was unmatched for the era, because their process could build a large merchant ship in just one day. Ford took the concept and modernised it for the industrial age. On 1 December 1913, Ford opened the first assembly line system to mass-produce his automobiles. Determined to always be in the lead of the automobile industry, Ford reduced the time that it took to produce a vehicle from twelve hours to only two and a half hours. His goal was to produce 1,000 cars per day. The parts could be created quickly enough, but assembly was time consuming. Ford's assembly line concept made his dream a reality. The idea of each person doing a dedicated task helped the workforce become specialised, and therefore more efficient, in his or her job. This took the skillset of each worker down to one specific job, instead of many, which affected them when, and if, they chose to move on and work somewhere else. There were some that felt the assembly line removed the skill from the process and served to dehumanise the worker. The turnover rate in Ford's factory was high, because the work was so repetitive. The cost to retrain and make a worker efficient was so high that Ford needed to take drastic action to maintain his process and costs.

The method by which Henry Ford treated his work force is also something to note. It was a vast improvement compared to the rough conditions that workers had experienced previously. Ford expected dedication and hard work, but he felt that to keep turnaround low it was necessary to raise the wages paid in his factory. In the year 1913 Ford had to hire 52,000 workers, but managed to retain only 14,000. The efforts required to train new workers were expensive and time consuming, causing issues with the workflow in the factory. Henry Ford made history on 5 January 5 1914 when he doubled his worker's wages to $5 per day (approximately $119 or £82 today). This doubling of wages was a move that was unheard of for the era and made Ford's factory the place that all of the top talent wanted to work. Ford also reduced the hours in the workday from nine to eight. The announcement had a huge impact, because the very next day over 10,000 workers lined-up outside of Ford's factory looking for work. The move made international news, spawning thirty-five articles in the *New York Times* alone. On the other side of this coin, Ford was actually viciously opposed to labour unions.

A brief history of Ford's efforts towards the workforce could seem like a win-win for everyone, except that, as with so much of Henry Ford, digging a little deeper unveils a more complicated view of the man and his methods and how they often seemed to circle back to his distrust of immigrants. The $5 per day wasn't a wage that you would just walk off the street and get. It was actually an incentive wage and wasn't guaranteed unless you met Ford's rigorous requirements. Ford required his immigrant workforce to attend the company English school in order to become fully 'Americanised'. It took six months to graduate 'the pageant of the Ford melting pot'. The workers who completed the forced cultural appropriation training would all dress in stereotypical clothing from their country of origin and jump into a literal large pot and get stirred-up. The workers would then emerge wearing a proper American-style suit and a straw hat. It must have been quite a spectacle. The idea of Americanisation was far from something that Henry Ford invented. In fact, Americans had been practising a form of cultural assimilation when it came to Native Americans for hundreds of years prior to that. The idea behind it was to 'civilize' the Native Americans and adapt them to the European-American way of life, customs, clothing and education. This bigoted and ignorant process would effectively nullify their culture.

The Ford Sociological Department would also be sent to invade the personal lives of the workers to investigate the cleanliness of their homes. In KGB-like fashion, they would grill the workers to find out whether they sent money back to anyone 'back home', if they were really married, did they have any boarders in the house, and would even check to see if their water was clean. Henry Ford tried to socially engineer immigrants to force them to become his vision of an American citizen. It turns out that Ford actually used his $5 a day wage as a way to strip the foreign culture out of immigrants. After two failed inspections a worker was fired. That level of invasion of privacy and social engineering would be unheard of in today's world.

Henry Ford eventually embarked on a massive public relations campaign, even going to the lengths of establishing the Ford Motion Picture Department to produce in-house features. It was in 1914 that they released their first movie in theatres titled *How Henry Ford Makes 1000 Cars A Day*. The self-promoting film presented Henry Ford as a simple everyman with simple tastes. Henry Ford was portrayed as hard working, like his workers, and a plain man that just likes to work on his farm.

The real Henry Ford was a peculiar dichotomy, he was a very wealthy man that was often photographed with his many celebrity friends and yet he enjoyed a reputation in the press as the everyman industrialist. This treatment would cause the ego of Henry Ford to grow. When it came to dealing with his employees, his ego would never allow him to fire anyone himself; that could damage his image. Instead, he would have the unsavoury task done on the sly. An employee could come in for work one day and their desk would have simply disappeared. Ford came to enjoy the power that he held over others, a position that would swell his own self-importance and convince him that his own judgement and opinions were impeccable and not to be questioned.

The Ford Motor Company Changes Hands

Henry Ford begrudgingly handed over the Ford Motor Company to his son Edsel in 1918, but that was far from the last time he would be involved in the decision making process. Ford would retain a high level of control in the company, eventually even tricking the stockholders into selling their shares to him and Edsel, which placed the control of the company back in the hands of the Ford family. Truly, Henry Ford would let Edsel only ostensibly run the company, while he continued to control and manipulate every aspect and even take the opportunity to humiliate Edsel from time to time.

The 1920s in America were full of change. There was new youthful music, dancing clubs and prohibition. The change was all over the roadways. There were suddenly so many cars, where there had been virtually none before. The roadways were often clogged and congested, but this new era brought an enormous amount of change. The automobile industry boom fuelled the rubber and oil industries, created gas stations, roadside motels, restaurants and of course the inevitable road construction and expansion. The sudden boom and use of the car changed vacation habits and even the way cities were set up. The younger generation had embraced the idea of the car as a tool of leisure and escape, a fact that the old fashioned thinker Henry Ford wasn't fond of. The new generation of consumers would demand more detailed and flashy cars, along with new features. The Roaring Twenties were full of flash and style, a trend that Ford had no intention of carrying over into his own vehicles. The flagrant consumerism seemed to make him uncomfortable. 'The American of a generation ago was a shrewd buyer', Ford said, 'but nowadays the American people seem to listen and be sold.'

Ford ignored the new marketplace and the inevitable happened…sales began to fall. The sales of Chevy/GM, by contrast, had tripled and were available in a variety of fresh, new colours. Ford didn't want to make anything but the Model T. He held strong to the idea that his own vision was all that mattered, and it began to hold him back in the marketplace. The Model T had already become obsolete in the new world. Ford asserted, 'The only problem with a Ford car is that we can't produce it fast enough'.

Edsel Ford saw the need to make some major changes and finally went toe-to-toe with his father. The sleek Ford Model A was the first Ford car to be available on an instalment plan. Edsel was behind it, but Ford took the credit in the press. Edsel had to push to get it made. The Model A revived the company's sales, with 700,000 cars sold in the first year alone. The relationship between Henry Ford and his son soured at this point, and would never properly recover. Henry couldn't face that his baby, the Model T, was now obsolete; but the country was going through a major period of change. Rural America began to disappear, as more people were living in cities than on the farm.

The 1929 Stock Market crash deeply affected the city of Detroit and the auto industry. A wave of poverty and unemployment began to move across the country and soon the consumer was no longer there. In four years the automobile marketplace lost ninety per cent of its previous business. Ford tried to keep the workers solvent and raised wages to $7 per day, but Model A sales weren't there anymore, so the layoffs came. The mayor of Detroit, Frank Murphy, estimated in the early 1930s that a third of the 200,000 people in the bread lines were laid off by Ford's factories alone. Unemployed citizens would wait hours for just a small ration of bread during the difficult economic times. The former employees of Ford were hungry and would even take to the streets with other unemployed workers in hunger marches. An article published in *Fortune* at the time noted that 'Declining sales have changed Mr Ford from one of the greatest U.S. money-makers to one of the greatest money losers.' Ironically, the very same *Fortune* magazine would name Henry Ford as businessman of the century in 1999.

Henry Ford and the Unions

Henry Ford hated the idea of a labour union. He hated that they were a challenge to his power and his absolute authority over the way he chose to run his factory.

Ford employed a young man named Harry Bennett, an ex-Navy man, to control the River Rouge factory floor with his gang of armed toughs that kept strict grips on the employees. Bennett was a small man at only 5ft 7in, and weighing a spry 145lbs. Ford wanted the 24-year-old to act as his muscle at his Rouge factory. The men there were gritty and tough to manage and Ford needed someone who answered directly to him that could strong-arm the employees into subservience. Bennett wasn't a disappointment; he and his men ruled the plant with an iron fist and loaded weapons.

Bennett kept a basement office at the Rouge, which included a secret door that could be opened by using a button underneath his desk. In this secret room, Bennett and Ford would have their meetings, with a guarantee of the utmost privacy. Bennett was a company man through and through, once boasting, 'I am Mr Ford's personal man.' His dedication to Henry Ford was second to none. 'If Mr Ford told me to blacken out the sun tomorrow, I might have trouble fixing it. But you'd see a hundred thousand sons-of-bitches coming through the Rouge gates in the morning, all wearing dark glasses.'

Bennett played the role of a gentleman gangster, recruiting a variety of athletes, ex-military and even ex-cons to his Ford enforcement department, dubbed the Service Department. The men, adorned with suits, fedoras and guns, used the threat of physical violence to keep the workforce in check. The rules in the factories became strict and overbearing. The workers weren't allowed to talk to each other or even sit down. The workers became accustomed to the absurd rules that they even learned to speak to each other without moving their lips, hoping to avoid a beating at the hands of Bennett and his men. The workers referred to it as the 'Fordization of the face'.

The National Labor Relations Act, also known as the Wagner Act, was passed in 1935. This new legal foundation gave workers the right to organise into unions, giving them the power to negotiate working conditions and wages. The Ford Motor Company was one of the last big companies to fight the unions. Bennett was authorised by Ford to take care of the union by any means necessary. The Service Department thugs attacked the union representatives when they came to the factory to hand out pamphlets. Images taken by photographers on the scene were soon published around the United States, showing evidence of the brutal nature of the battle that the unions were fighting. The restrictions in the Ford factory got out of control for a time. At one point, if men were seen talking in groups they were assumed to be unionising, were often beaten and subsequently fired. In April of 1941, 50,000 Ford workers protested outside the Rouge plant, pressing Ford to give in to the union demands for pay and conditions. Ford reportedly fumed that he would rather shut down his factory than give in to the union demands, but even Ford couldn't ultimately stop the union. Ford's son Edsel would step in as the voice of reason and strike a deal with the union, a move that Ford would resent.

Bennett became the trusted right-hand man of Henry Ford, which was likely a sore spot for his son, Edsel. When one man threatened Edsel's life,

Bennett assured him that he would handle the situation and the man turned up dead shortly thereafter. Bennett was clearly not a person to be crossed. Henry Ford eventually had Bennett spy on his son, who was living a lush extravagant lifestyle, which Ford hated. Edsel, an only son, soon began to see Bennett as a rival for his father's affections, something that he gave out in very short supply as it was.

The Henry Ford who employed Bennett to control his workers was a far cry from the younger Henry Ford, who had been an eager pioneer and business mogul. No, this Ford was increasingly paranoid and angry. Ford felt that the world he knew was gone and that the country had lost control; he would often comment about how he yearned for yesterday. Ford didn't mellow as he aged either, he continued to insist that the Jews were persecuting him and Edsel became concerned for his father's state of mind and his ability to run the Ford Motor Company. Ford did suffer two mild strokes, one in 1938 and another in 1941; in 1945 however, he had another, far more severe, stroke that left him in a state of mental confusion. Edsel had died of stomach cancer on 26 May 1943, aged 49, so his son, Henry Ford II, took over as president of the Ford Motor Company. Henry Ford died on 7 April 1947 at the age of 83.

The Rampant Anti-Semitism of the Era

Around a million Jews lived in the United States at the dawn of the twentieth century; half were located in New York City. This is a stark contrast to the previous Jewish population in America, which had been 50,000 only a half-century before. The population would continue to grow rapidly with 1.75 million Jews immigrating to America between 1900 and 1924. The power and influence of the Jewish community in society and in politics began to grow significantly during this time, as they began to represent 3.5 per cent of the American populace. This was a huge change from the less than 1 per cent that Jews had represented prior to this era. In fact, the primarily East Coast Jewish population was such a presence that when Theodore Roosevelt was running for his first full term presidency in 1904, his campaign released pamphlets in Yiddish.

The Jewish presence had become so noticeably large in America that by the time the First World War rolled around, the armed forces began to cater especially to the Jewish population, trying to incite them to get involved in the war effort. On 9 April 1917, the Jewish Welfare Board was established, a mere three days after America officially declared its war on Germany. The purpose of the JWB was to support Jewish soldiers during wartime and to recruit and train rabbis, in much the same way that priests and pastors were provided to support the Christian soldiers.

It was during the time between the First World War and the Second World War that anti-Semitism would grow rapidly in the United States. The conditions of the Great Depression would exacerbate the growing resentment, and even violence, towards the American Jewish population, due to a perception that wealthy Jews and Jewish bankers were responsible for the stock market crash.

Another major opposition to the Jews at the time was the Ku Klux Klan. The first rise of the KKK was reactionary following the loss of the South to the North in the American Civil War. The KKK would only last for five years during that volatile era of American history, but would rise again in 1915 and last all the way to 1944, near the end of the Second World War. The original incarnation of the KKK was directly opposed to African American leaders and advancement, and while the second version was no fan of African Americans, their focus was more on the recent immigrants to the United States, focusing on Jews and Catholics. The numbers of the Klan grew exponentially, clocking in at over 4 million, far surpassing the entire Jewish population of America at the time.

One of the darker stories of anti-Semitism to come from pre-war America was the lynching of a Jewish businessman, Leo Frank, in Atlanta back in 1915. Frank was accused of murdering a worker in the pencil factory that he managed. The then governor of Georgia, John M. Slaton, commuted Frank's sentence to life in prison instead of death row. This pardoning of a Jew incited a rabid mob that proceeded to break into the jail, drag Frank out into the street, and hang him. Evidence that was later brought to light showed that the very man who accused Frank of the crime, the pencil plant janitor Jim Conley, might have been responsible for the crime himself. Frank was given a posthumous pardon for the murder in 1986.

Although there were isolated examples of actual physical violence, the climate had certainly turned against the Jewish immigrants in the United States. The results of a 1938 Gallup poll revealed that fifty per cent of Americans, when questioned, answered 'yes' to having a low opinion of Jews. That is where American society was at the onset of the Second World War.

This was an era when the New International Encyclopaedia had the following entry describing Jews as a race:

Among the distinguishing mental and moral traits of the Jews may be mentioned: distaste for hard or violent physical labor; a strong family sense and philoprogenitiveness; a marked religious instinct; the courage of the prophet and martyr rather than of the pioneer and soldier; remarkable power to survive in adverse environments, combined with great ability to retain racial solidarity; capacity for exploitation, both individual and social; shrewdness and astuteness in speculation and money matters generally; an Oriental love of display and a full appreciation of the power and pleasure of social position; a very high average of intellectual ability.

The fact that an entire race of people is 'defined' or stereotyped in such a manner is yet another example of the way society at the time thought of the Jewish people; as their own race that required a separate definition.

The Dearborn Independent Years

It was in the year 1918 that Henry Ford had Ernest G. Liebold, his private secretary, purchase *The Dearborn Independent*, a local weekly newspaper based in Dearborn, Michigan. Ford invested a whopping five million dollars in the newspaper, which allowed him to project his own voice and views into the populace. The original editor of the paper refused to print Ford's anti-Semitic essays, so he fired him and hired a new editor who would be happy to comply. In the paper, Ford would publish articles about a vast and secret worldwide conspiracy of Jewish control and manipulation. During its peak the circulation of the newspaper was a staggering 700,000 readers. It was sold by subscription and more than 7,000 Ford dealerships nationwide were required to carry it, thus ensuring that Ford's right-wing mouthpiece had a wide reach. It was far from the only anti-Semitic paper, but this one had a circulation across the country.

The Dearborn Independent would publish its very first anti-Semitic article titled: *Anti-Semitism – Will It Appear in the United States?* The article, which does not list any specific author, addresses what they call the 'Jewish Question' in the United States. The article proceeds to define what they consider to be the four types of Jews and complains that anyone who questions the very presence and intentions of Jews in America (the Jewish Question) is considered to be hateful and anti-Semitic:

It is not recognition of the Jewish Question. If it were, then it could be set down that the bulk of the American people arc destined to become anti-Semites, for they are beginning to recognise the existence of a Jewish

Question and will steadily do so in increasing numbers as the Question is forced upon them from the various practical angles of their lives. The Question is here. We may be honestly blind to it. We may be timidly silent about it. We may even make dishonest denial of it. But it is here. In time all will have to recognise it. In time the polite 'hush,hush' of oversensitive or intimidated circles will not be powerful enough to suppress it. But to recognise it will not mean that we have gone over to a campaign of hatred and enmity against the Jews. It will only mean that a stream of tendency which has been flowing through our civilisation has at last accumulated bulk and power enough to challenge attention, to call for some decision with regard to it, to call for the adoption of a policy which will not repeat the mistakes of the past and yet will forestall any possible social menace of the future.

A selection of these anti-Semitic articles and editorials would later be collected into book format in 1920 under the title *The International Jew – The World's Foremost Problem*. Ford would go on to distribute half a million copies of his anti-Semitic opus through his car dealerships and nationwide subscribers to the *Dearborn Independent*. *The International Jew* was a book that Adolf Hitler himself would own and would become a bestseller in Nazi-era Germany. The book would also spawn a second volume in April of 1921, *Jewish Activities in the United States: Volume II of The International Jew*.

Ford's anti-Semitic book may have been a smash-hit in Nazi Germany, but there was certainly a vocal resistance to it back home in America. *The International Jew*, along with other similar publications and pamphlets, inspired the Federal Council of Churches of Christ in America to publish an anti-propaganda statement titled *The Peril of Racial Prejudice*. The document was signed by dozens of clergy, authors, journalists and even politicians. In fact, the first name at the top of the list was the then sitting President, Woodrow Wilson, himself. The document expressed a cooperative concern about the rampant spread of anti-Semitic materials and sentiment:

The undersigned citizens of Gentile birth and Christian faith, view with profound regret and disapproval the appearance in this country of what is apparently an organized campaign of anti-Semitism, conducted in close conformity to and co-operation with similar campaigns in Europe. We regret exceedingly the publication of a number of books, pamphlets and newspaper articles designed to foster distrust and suspicion of our fellow-citizens of Jewish ancestry and faith–distrust and suspicion of their loyalty and their patriotism.

These publications, to which wide circulation is being given, are thus introducing into our national political life a new and dangerous spirit, one that is wholly at variance with our traditions and ideals and subversive of our system of government.

The Dearborn Independent would make a point of running stories that attacked certain prominent members of the Jewish business community by name. The newspaper would blame the Jews for anything from the First World War to illegal bootlegging, Jazz music and even the Bolshevik Revolution. Henry Ford's mouthpiece would make a misstep when they published the inflammatory *The Story of the Sapiro Boys*. The paranoid articles would accuse the agricultural cooperative movement, which was headed by Aaron Sapiro, of defrauding American farmers in the name of a mythical international Jewish conspiracy that was looking to takeover and seize the agricultural and horticultural resources of America and try to starve American citizens.

Ford's Anti-Semitic Writings

Henry Ford firmly believed what was quickly becoming a national consensus at the time, that all of the money dealers in the world, from Wall Street to the Bankers, were Jewish and seeking total control over all Americans. He believed that Jews cheated everyone in business and were merciless profiteers. Jews became a symbol of manipulation and control to Ford, and the source of all the problems of the world. 'If there is one quality that attracts Jews, it is power', Ford wrote in *The Dearborn Independent*. 'The Jews are the scavengers of the world. Wherever there's anything wrong with a country, you'll find the Jews on the job there.' The Jewish people have been the popular scapegoats for the world's problems for a long time, without much of a pushback from more progressive individuals. It's only after the horrific events of the Second World War and the Holocaust that the world was able to recognise the evils of anti-Semitism in any serious way.

Ford made a distinction between what he saw as the two types of Jews, the poor Jew and the 'International Jew'. The International Jew is seen as a predatory archetype that Ford describes as a 'rich exploiter of his race'. Henry Ford believed that there was a complete justification for what he considered to be an intelligent and rational form of anti-Semitism based on his own paranoia about the International Jew:

The Jew is again being singled out for critical attention throughout the world. His emergence in the financial, political and social spheres has been so complete and spectacular since the war, that his place, power and purpose in the world are being given a new scrutiny, much of it unfriendly.

Ford seemed to operate on the philosophy that if an idea, no matter how bad or wicked, is popular enough or thought to be true by enough individuals then it's valid. This is the same logic that would create a horrific reality for so many in Germany years later under the rule of the Nazi regime.

Ford would also reprint an inflammatory and notorious anti-Semitic text from 1903 that had its origins in Russia, *The Protocols of the Elders of Zion*. This forged set of documents detailed the vast, imaginary, international Jewish conspiracy that Ford himself would adamantly assert was real. The basic idea was that there was an elite group of wealthy and powerful Jews who controlled the fates of the world. An abridged version of the documents would be included in article form in *The Dearborn Independent* and eventually in the contents of his book, *The International Jew*.

Despite the fact that *The Times* of London had already exposed *The Protocols of the Elders of Zino* as completely false in 1921, Ford would continue to publish the contents of the document. *The Protocols* would go on to be taught as absolute fact in children's classrooms throughout Nazi Germany. In fact, prior to the Second World War, the National Socialist Party would reprint *The Protocols* twenty-three times. In his public apology that was issued in 1927 (discussed later in this chapter), Ford would acknowledge *The Protocols* as 'gross forgeries'.

On 29 May 1920, Ford published an editorial on the topic of the German outlook on the topic of Jews and the blame he felt they carried for the state of things in Germany after the First World War. He starts the article by stating:

Humanity has become wise enough to discuss those forms of physical sickness over which it formerly drew the veil of shame and secrecy, but political hygiene is not so far advanced. The main source of the sickness of the German national body is charged to be the influence of the Jews, and although this was apparent to acute minds years ago, it is now said to have gone so far as to be apparent to the least observing. The eruption has broken out on the surface of the body politic, and no further concealment of this fact is possible. It is the belief of all classes of the German people that the collapse which has come since the armistice, and the revolution from which they are being prevented a recovery, are the result of Jewish intrigue and purpose. Ford didn't believe that Jews had any place in German society,

The Jew in Germany is regarded as only a guest of the people, Ford wrote, *...he has offended by trying to turn himself into the host. There are no stronger contrasts in the world than the pure Germanic and pure Semitic races; therefore, there has been no harmony between the two in Germany; the German has regarded the Jew strictly as a guest, while the Jew, indignant at not being given the privileges of the nation-family, has cherished animosity against his host.*

One pervasive theme throughout Ford's writing is something he calls the 'Jewish Question'. He discusses in-depth his feeling that Jews weren't being discriminated against or singled-out due to their religion, but rather due to the attitude of inclusiveness involved in Jewish culture and various attributes that he considers a part of their genetic make-up as an ethnicity.

In today's world the question of political correctness is often a hot-button issue, especially in America. There is a firm divide between people who believe in sensitivity and dignity for all and those who believe speech, and the way we address things like gender, sexuality, race and religion, should not be altered at all with modern terminology or progressive ways of thinking. This can often lead to labels and attitudes that many find offensive. It's clear from Ford's writing that racial sensitivity was an issue of debate even back in the 1920s, particularly when it pertains to anti-Semitism:

The chief difficulty in writing about the Jewish Question is the super sensitiveness of Jews and non-Jews concerning the whole matter. There is a vague feeling that even to openly use the word 'Jew,' or to expose it nakedly to print, is somehow improper. Polite evasions like 'Hebrew' and 'Semite', both of which are subject to the criticism of inaccuracy, are timidly essayed, and people pick their way gingerly as if the whole subject were forbidden, until some courageous Jewish thinker comes straight out with the good old word 'Jew', and then the constraint is relieved and the air cleared.

There is extreme sensitiveness about the public discussion of the Jewish Question on the part of Gentiles...the Jew still remains the enigma of the world.

Ford was increasingly obsessed with his conspiracy theories. He was convinced that the 'Jewish Question' comes down to the power and control that he claims the Jews were seeking around the world:

> *Is there a Jewish Question in Russia? Unquestionably, in its most virulent form...Whether you go to Rumania, Russia, Austria or Germany, or anywhere else that the Jewish Question has come to the forefront as a vital issue, you will discover that the principal cause is the outworking of the Jewish genius to achieve the power of control.*

Ford goes on to describe his view of the Jewish people:

> *The Jew is the world's enigma. Poor in his masses, he yet controls the world's finances. Scattered abroad without country or government, he yet presents a unity of race continuity which no other people has achieved. Living under legal disabilities in almost every land, he has become the power behind many a throne. There are ancient prophecies to the effect that the Jew will return to his own land and from that centre rule the world, though not until he has undergone an assault by the united nations of mankind.*

Ford and his newspaper were getting a lot of negative feedback about his articles highlighting what he considered the threat of the 'International Jew', and he was less than sensitive to their concerns in reply. When faced with mass criticism of the outright racist and hateful nature of the articles in his newspaper, Ford actually managed to take the stance of the victim:

> *This series of articles is already being met by an organized barrage by mail and wire and voice, every single item of which carries the wail of persecution. One would think that a heartless and horrible attack were being made on a most pitiable and helpless people – until one looks at the letterheads of the magnates who write, and at the financial ratings of those who protest, and at the membership of the organizations whose responsible heads hysterically demand retraction. And always in the background there is the threat of boycott, a threat which has practically sealed up the columns of every publication in America against even the mildest discussion of the Jewish Question.*
>
> *The Jewish Question in America cannot be concealed forever by threats against publications, nor by the propagandist publication of*

matter extremely and invariably favorable to everything Jewish. It is here and it cannot be twisted into something else by the adroit use of propaganda, nor can it be forever silenced by threats. The Jews of the United States can best serve themselves and their fellow-Jews all over the world by letting drop their far too ready cry of 'anti-Semitism...'

Henry Ford - The Ignorant Anarchist

It could be assumed that Henry Ford was a brilliant man, because of the immense impact that his business had on the world, but to do so would be getting ahead of ourselves. Ford was cunning, ruthless, driven and certainly inventive. It's not uncommon for someone to be highly gifted in an area of life and ignorant in many others. Henry Ford was an under-educated farm boy and a lot of his ideas about society and the world may have been skewed by this fact. Evidence of Henry Ford's lack of comprehension came to light in 1919, when he sued the *Chicago Tribune* for libel.

The strides that Ford made for his workforce and the immense, self-promoting marketing campaign he embarked on certainly worked wonders on his public image. Henry Ford was used to being the darling of most columnists and writers, so much so that he couldn't deal well with anything but being unconditionally beloved. When Henry Ford opposed American military action in Mexico, he began to find criticism in the pages of the *Chicago Tribune*. The *Tribune* was in support of drafting men into the National Guard, even vowing to hold jobs for anyone called to duty, while the pacifist Henry Ford refused to do so. An article with the headline: 'Henry Ford is an Anarchist' called Ford an 'ignorant idealist' and an anarchist-enemy of the nation. This accusations enfuriated Ford and he decided to fight back in court.

Ford took the *Chicago Tribune* to court, seeking one million dollars in damages. The trial began in the summer of 1919 and took fourteen weeks to present each side. It was during this trial that the ignorance and weak character of Henry Ford became evident. One observer, author John Tebbel, reflected on Ford's testimony: 'He was virtually illiterate, obviously, and his philosophy was unashamedly out of the cracker barrel.' This was a very telling insult to Ford's intelligence. The use of the term 'cracker barrel' refers to the old barrels of crackers that would be in the local country stores during the late nineteenth century. The stereotype is that the plain and simple country folk would gather there to talk, much like the 'water cooler' is used as a reference today. Cracker barrel philosophy was thought to be the inane ramblings of ignorant rural citizens.

The primary lawyer for the *Tribune*, Elliott K. Stevenson, began to ask Ford a number of questions on American history, in order to establish his level of ignorance and validating the newspaper's position on his intelligence. Among the absurdities, Henry Ford was found to believe that the Revolutionary War occurred in 1812, and thought that notorious traitor Benedict Arnold was a writer. It has been said that copies of Ford's testimony were printed and sold near the courthouse, inspiring an immense amount of laughter and mockery from the public. The entire experience served only to show a wilful ignorance in Ford. Ford refused to read in front of the jury, making excuses about forgetting his glasses and that his eyes watering; when asked if he wanted to leave the jury with the impression that he was illiterate, Ford is said to have replied: 'Yes, you can leave it that way.' Throughout the eight days of questioning, Henry Ford would often lose interest and wander around the courtroom, looking out the windows and fidgeting. He was clearly out of his league in the proceedings.

The jury, which consisted primarily of farmers, did find for Henry Ford in the end. They awarded him the amount of six whole cents after a ten-hour deliberation.

Henry Ford and *The Dearborn Independent* are Sued

In 1927, Jewish lawyer and farm cooperative organiser Aaron Sapiro brought a lawsuit against Henry Ford accusing him of defamation for his many years of clearly anti-Semitic articles in *The Dearborn Independent*. This was the third lawsuit of this kind that had been raised against the newspaper, but the only one that would end up going to trial. Ford would not testify at the trial, but instead faked a car accident and hid out in the hospital to avoid it. Ford would then issue a less than sincere apology and shut down *The Dearborn Independent* for good. The final issue was published on 31 December 1927.

Ford wrote a statement of apology to be released on 30 June 1927, regarding '*Charges Against Jews Made in His Publications, The Dearborn Independent and a Series of Pamphlets Entitled The 'International Jew'*. In this apology letter he defers responsibility of the newspaper's anti-Jew articles to his underlings and basically denies the reality that he was the mastermind behind the racist newspaper:

> *For some time past I have given consideration to the series of articles concerning Jews which since 1920 have appeared in The Dearborn Independent. Some of them have been reprinted in pamphlet form under*

the title 'The International Jew'. Although both publications are my property, it goes without saying that in the multitude of my activities it has been impossible for me to devote personal attention to their management or to keep informed as to their contents. It has therefore inevitably followed that the conduct and policies of these publications had to be delegated to men whom I placed in charge of them and upon whom I relied implicitly.

In an even more nervy move, Ford goes on to paint himself in a sympathetic manner towards Jews, while subsequently claiming that he had no idea that his newspaper was publishing his own editorials and collecting them in book format for distribution at his own dealerships and worldwide readership:

To my great regret I have learned that Jews generally, and particularly those of this country, not only resent these publications as promoting anti-Semitism, but regard me as their enemy. Trusted friends with whom I have conferred recently have assured me in all sincerity that in their opinion the character of the charges and insinuations made against the Jews, both individually and collectively, contained in many of the articles which have been circulated periodically in The Dearborn Independent and have been reprinted in the pamphlets mentioned, justifies the righteous indignation entertained by Jews everywhere toward me because of the mental anguish occasioned by the unprovoked reflections made upon them.

Henry Ford ordered the remaining copies of his horrible anti-Semitic book to be burned and the production of future copies ceased. The sad reality is that by then, Ford had already used his considerable authority and influence as a cultural icon to legitimise his racist ideals. A lot of Jewish organisations at the time accepted Ford's apology as sincere, especially since he shut the paper down, but it would later be revealed in the accounts of those that knew him that Henry Ford still firmly held his views behind closed doors, as evidenced by his ongoing involvement financially and publicly with the Nazi Party.

Henry Ford, Hitler and the Nazi Party

Henry Ford had conquered the automobile marketplace in America, with the majority of all car sales split between the 'Big Three': Ford, GM and Chrysler by the late 1920s. The American marketplace was an important mountain to climb, but once that was dominated, it was time for the 'big three' to set their sights elsewhere in the world; one such place was Germany. Ford had begun to have a German presence in 1912, when they began manufacturing parts in Hamburg. Ford soon began manufacturing in Berlin and on 1 April 1926, the very first German built Model T was assembled. Ford moved its manufacturing facilities to Cologne in 1931, and built a facility right on the banks of the Rhine, providing waterway access between it and other Ford facilities such as Manchester and Dagenham in Britain.

Meanwhile, a young Adolf Hitler was spending hours in his rented room, reading book after book, developing his thoughts on the world and society. One of the things he read was the work of one of the most wealthy and recognisable celebrities in America – Henry Ford. Hitler had access to the four volumes of *The International Jew* and he held Ford's work in high esteem.

Hitler published his own manifesto on 18 July 1925, the now notorious book *Mein Kampf*, which translates as *My Struggle*. The 720 page book was dictated by Hitler while he was behind bars, serving time for his treasonous but failed coup attempt called the Munich Putsch. Hitler and his Nazi Party tried to seize power in Germany by force, a goal that they would later achieve more through political manipulation. Hitler's jail time wasn't spent the way one might imagine; as leader of the National Socialist Party, he was already something of a people's folk hero in Germany. He received excellent treatment, had comfortable accommodation and enjoyed many visitors during his time in prison.

Mein Kampf would include plans for Germany's future, observations on culture and, most importantly, groundwork for an anti-Semitic platform that would define the rest of Hitler's life. There are early suggestions of genocide as an option for dealing with the Jewish people, whom he felt to be inferior. *Mein Kampf* is an important time stamp in the life of Henry Ford, because he is the one and only American mentioned by name in the hate text. Hitler mentions *The Dearborn Independent* newspaper articles on the Jewish conspiracy by name and heralds Ford as: 'one great man, Ford, to their exasperation still holds out independently there even now', referring to Ford's resistance of his perceived Jewish control over the American economy and manufacturing. This mention is a powerful insight not only into how vicious and dangerous the anti-Semitic rhetoric propagated by Henry Ford was, but also how far reaching it was. It cannot be underplayed that Henry Ford's anti-Semitism inspired Adolf Hitler himself; what a powerful and destructive legacy to leave in one's wake.

If the connection between Hitler and Ford ended with *The Dearborn Independent* and a mention in *Mein Kampf* it would be more than enough to tarnish a legacy, but alas the story is far from over. Henry Ford and his son Edsel played a role in the Second World War that is certainly questionable and is the source of fierce debate. Ostensibly, the control of the German Ford plants were placed under German control during the war, as they would be nearly impossible to run from America during that era, but whenever vital elements such as rubber were needed, they went through the American Ford division.

The German government didn't regard Hitler and his Nazi party as an idle threat. In fact, over a decade before Hitler managed to seize complete power, the German government was already taking steps against him and his 'beer hall' political movement. There was also a feeling among some areas of the German population that something wasn't right with the National Socialist Movement. An article in the *New York Times*, which ran in December of 1922, bore the title 'Berlin Hears Ford Is Backing Hitler'. The article details the concern brought to the attention of the American Ambassador in Berlin by the renowned German newspaper, *Berlin Tageblatt*, that Ford was financing Hitler. The feeling was that Hitler's lavish accommodation in Munich, highly paid lieutenants and the funds the Nazi party was enjoying were more far-reaching than could be provided solely by contributions from local German citizens. The article goes on to note that Hitler and his men were seen driving two brand new automobiles, that the wall next to Hitler's desk in Munich had a large portrait of Henry Ford, and owned many translated copies of Ford's books in his chambers.

A 1931 interview given by Hitler to *Detroit News* reporter Annetta Antona generated another infamous quote about Henry Ford. During the interview, Antona asked Hitler why he had a portrait of Henry Ford next to his desk, to which Hitler replied 'I regard Henry Ford as my inspiration.'

Henry Ford would become the source of great controversy yet again in 1938 when he accepted the Grand Cross of the German Eagle, the highest honour that the Nazi party could bestow upon a foreigner. The flashy medal consisted of an iron cross, flanked by four Nazi swastikas. There was a backlash to this in the United States, as the event was well publicised by newspapers such as the *New York Times*. Protestors could be found outside of Ford plants carrying signs with statements like: 'Why Did Ford Get A Nazi Medal?' The event also served to cause a few diplomatic issues between the United States and Germany at the time. The events were temporary, but the impact was definitely felt.

Ford and Forced Labour

The Ford manufacturing activities in Germany would soon fall under the name Ford-Werke in 1939. The French and German Ford manufacturing facilities would go on to produce not only vehicles and weaponry for the Nazi German military forces throughout the Second World War, but would use forced labour to do so. In fact, the forced labour aspect was in effect long before the start of the war and even before Ford-Werke was separated from the American Ford Motor Company. Forced labour was far from unique in Nazi-controlled Germany. There are reports that upwards of 7.5 million people were forced to relocate from their various conquered homelands to Germany and to work without compensation in order to keep the Nazi war machine running smoothly.

A lawsuit was brought to court in New Jersey in 1998 by Elsa Iwanowa, one of the survivors that was ripped from her home and forced to work at Ford-Werke. The Ford Motor Company went to court and acknowledged Iwanowa's claims and validated the forced labour, but denied any responsibility for the American wing of the company. The word at the time was that, even after the Second World War began, the American wing of Ford Motor Company still owned a majority stock in Ford-Werke. The lawsuit never got a chance to be fully realised, since it was dismissed in 1999. The statue of limitations to raise a suit of that nature had unfortunately expired.

The Ford Legacy

When Henry Ford died on 7 April 1947, over one hundred thousand citizens made their way to his funeral and waited for several hours in a queue for a chance to view the body of the legendary Henry Ford. Today, Henry Ford is remembered as an influential industrialist and an American icon that changed the course of history. The people have turned Henry Ford into a heroic and immortal figure in history, often choosing to forget the very human and flawed man behind the brand name.

The image of the Ford Motor Company began to change when the grandson of Henry Ford, Henry Ford II, took over control of the company in 1945. One of his first acts as president was to fire Ford's sketchy 'muscle' and head of the Ford Service Department, Harry Bennett. He then set out to surround himself with experienced executives who assisted him in taking the company from the emotional brainchild of one man to a well-respected and long-lasting corporate entity. In 1956, the Ford Motor Company became a publicly traded corporation under the leadership of Henry Ford II.

The Ford Motor Company is a very different company today than it was a century ago. In one glaring example of this, the President and Chief Executive Officer of the company (at the time of writing this book) is a Jewish businessman named Mark Fields. The dark shadows of Henry Ford's legacy have been left far behind and instead the memory of his technological innovations remain. It would be hard to blame the modern day Ford Motor Company for wanting to brush the history of its founder under the rug in lieu of a legacy of hatred and bigotry.

Chapter Four

Adidas & Puma: Cogs in the Nazi War Machine

T he shoe has become its own fashion statement. Consumers often
pay big bucks for limited edition or fun new shoes. Sneakerheads, a
name given to shoe collectors, will even wait hours or even days in
line for limited edition new release 'kicks'. There are several popular names
in shoes, but none carry the nefarious history of Adidas and Puma. The
history behind these two companies is riddled with a bitter sibling rivalry
between two brothers who founded their fortunes while loyally serving the
Nazis.

Early Days of the Dassler Brothers

The Dassler brothers were born two years apart in their quaint hometown of
Herzogenaurach, Germany. Nestled quietly in the Middle Franconia region
of Bavaria, Herzogenaurach is located right on the Aurach River. Historically,
there was little reason to mention the sleepy town, not until it was made
famous by the Dassler brothers as the home base of their respective footwear
brand giants, Adidas and Puma. Rudolf, the founder of Puma, was the older
of the two brothers, born on 26 March 1898. The younger of the two, Adolf,
was born on 3 November 1900. Adolf was the founder and namesake for
his company, Adidas – a clever mixture of his nickname of 'Adi' and his last
name 'Dassler'. The brothers were two of the four children of Christoph
Von Wilhelm and Pauline Dassler. They also had another brother named
Fritz and a sister named Marie.

The industrious Adi would be the first brother to make a big move towards
the future. In the year 1920 he constructed a makeshift shoe production
studio in a shed that his mother had previously used for laundry. Adi had
only just returned from serving the German military in the First World
War and was already looking towards building a future for himself at home.
Christoph Dassler worked in a shoe factory to support his family, so the
move towards developing footwear was a natural one. Herzogenaurach was,
after all, a hotspot in Bavaria for shoemaking, boasting over one hundred
individual shoemakers in 1922. Christoph supported his son's endeavours as

Adi teamed with the Zehlein brothers, who were producing spikes for track shoes in their own blacksmithing workshop.

Rudolf eventually joined forces with his brother on 1 July 1924, when he and Adi established the Dassler Brothers Shoe Factory (translated from the German Gebrüder Dassler Schuhfabrik). Their goal was to create high-quality footwear for athletes of all kinds. It was a brave venture that the brothers undertook to open their own business in post First World War Germany. On the surface the brothers appeared to be a perfect match. Adi was the soft-spoken and thoughtful craftsman, a master of the workbench, while his brother Rudolf was a gregarious and outgoing salesman. Rudolf was very personable and easily mastered the commercial aspects of the business.

The Dassler brothers had a lot in common and got on quite well, although Rudolf had the assertive and dominant personality of an older sibling. As boys, Rudolf and Adi spent their spare time outdoors playing various sports, where there was always a healthy rivalry and sense of competition between them. Adi had the drive of a younger brother who wanted to outdo Rudolf in some realm and that realm was sports. No matter how hard Rudolf tried, he couldn't match Adi's natural talent and athleticism. Adi seemed to understand sport in a more organic way, which would end up translating into his ability to create and craft innovative sporting shoe designs.

Rudolf may not have been a master at sports and the physical, but he did consider himself to be a man of the world. In the early days of the business he was already a young father, husband and businessman. Rudolf married Friedl Strasser on 6 May 1928 and the couple had two sons, Armin and Gerd. Always seen carrying his pipe, he was quite popular with the ladies; his dapper, smooth confidence earned him a lot of affections outside of his marriage. He was well known as a lady-killer and it didn't amuse his wife Friedl one bit. Although she was well aware of his dalliances, he would usually hide them from her and engage in them while on holiday, sparing her embarrassment and pain. He didn't always keep to this way of doing things however; he once had an affair while she was pregnant, which destroyed her emotionally.

Rudolf may have been a ladies' man, but by contrast Adi was a bachelor through and through, that is until he met Käthe, the woman who would become his wife. The two married on 17 March 1934 and went on to have five children together; one son and four daughters. The two families of the Dassler brothers would become quite wealthy and well-to-do within their town, and their two families got along well for a time. The brothers found so much success under the Nazi regime that they soon needed larger factories to cope with the rapid growth. Rudolf's wife Friedl began to play a very active role in running the family business as a bookkeeper, but Adi's wife Käthe was less interested in the day-to-day operations.

Käthe was expected to participate and work, but she had only been 17 when she married Adi, and when their first child was born she refused to go to work. She lacked a work ethic, but had plenty of vision for what Adolf's role in the company should be. Käthe would eventually be the inspiration behind Adolf growing bold enough to move on his own. The two families moved into a joint house next to the factory, despite their personal differences. The families rarely got along and the Dassler brothers became increasingly bitter towards each other, though the subject of many of their early feuds is pure speculation. Adolf and his family resided on the ground floor; Rudolf and his family were on the next floor up and their parents above that. The close living quarters and stresses at work began to culminate in fighting and family disputes.

Nazi Germany

During the 1928 Olympic Games in Amsterdam the Dassler brothers equipped German athlete Lina Radke with her running shoes. Radke went on to be the very first athlete to win an Olympic gold medal for Germany. This accomplishment would reflect well on the Dassler brothers and brought some notoriety to their burgeoning company.

Fate would intervene in the lives of the Dasslers when Adolf Hitler and his National Socialist party assumed power of Germany in 1933. Adi and Rudolf both became members of the Nazi party, a practice that was not uncommon amongst German business owners, at least the ones that wanted to stay in business. It is also likely that Adi, as a veteran of the First World War, would have had strong feelings about the promises being touted by Adolf Hitler for rebuilding German society and the economy. The Dassler brothers, ever industrious, saw the opportunities that could come along with the new era of Aryan dominance sweeping through Germany. It wasn't long before the Swastika was all over their hometown of Herzogenaurach and the brothers weren't about to be left out of progress. In May 1933, focussing on what was best for the company at that time, the brothers officially joined the Nazi Party; it was a decision they would later come to regret. As party members however, the brothers were able to obtain a lot of benefits from the government and the Nazis were anxious to get young Germans involved in Nazi-approved sports to showcase their perceived physical superiority and Aryan prestige.

Fighting within the family may have begun, but by the summer of 1936 there was so much new business coming their way that the problems were kept at bay for a time. The Olympics were coming to Germany and with the Games came opportunity. The brothers would find an extreme level of notoriety when they convinced a young, would-be athlete to wear their shoes in the Olympic Games. The Dassler's set their sights on romancing American runner Jesse Owens well in advance and made a plan to get near him so they could offer him a pair of their custom, hand-made, running shoes.

Thanks to Hitler, the eyes of the world were closely focused on the Olympic Games that year and the brothers knew it was the perfect venue to showcase their product. Hitler had every intention of using the Olympics as his personal propaganda tool to show the world the grandeur and power of Nazi Germany. In an effort to add mystique and bravado to the games, the Nazis invented many of the ceremonial aspects of the Olympics that are still celebrated to this day. The first ever running of the torch and the grand opening ceremonies were both established by the Nazis. The eerie video and imagery from the 1936 games often shows crowds giving the Nazi salute with the Swastika banners looming in the background.

The Dasslers managed to work their way into the Olympic village in order to get close enough to Owens to convince the runner that their innovative shoes were the right ones to wear in the most important sports competition in the world. It turned out that Owens was indeed impressed with Adi's custom-fitted spiked shoe. Spikes had been around since 1890, when Reebok founder Joseph William Foster had introduced them to the United Kingdom. The Dassler shoes were so impressive that Owens allowed the Dasslers to fit the shoes directly to him.

Jesse Owens went on to bring home four gold medals for America. The sweeping victory made Owens famous and crushed Hitler's hopes of dominating the games with Aryan supremacy. Albert Speer, Hitler's chief architect, once recalled the Nazi leader's aggravation with Owens. Speer described Hitler as 'highly annoyed by the series of triumphs by the marvellous coloured American runner, Jesse Owens. People whose antecedents came from the jungle were primitive, Hitler said with a shrug; their physiques were stronger than those of civilised whites and hence should be excluded from future games.' This win was what would legitimise the footwear of the Dassler brothers and ensure their future. It was a bold move to provide Jesse Owens with footwear, to say the least, because it's not the kind of thing that would sit well with the Fuhrer. The Dasslers' business got a huge boost out of the experience, and Jesse Owens went on to be regarded as the sprinter of the century; something that the company would highlight in their advertising thereafter.

It wasn't long after those games that Nazi Germany began expanding their territory and became engulfed in all-out war. Inevitably, the landscape of the German economy began to change as the Second World War raged on. The only way Hitler could continue his reign of terror on Europe was to completely convert the whole of Germany into an industrial war complex. The 'total war' economy began to emerge, as all manufacturing began to move away from luxury items, and focussed instead on producing the various elements of war. In December of 1943 Hitler officially ordered all civilian business operations to cease and converted them to military manufacturing. The Dassler brothers were no longer creating sports shoes, but instead began to make boots for Nazi soldiers and Panzerschreck bazookas in their Herzogenaurach factory. The weaponry that the Dasslers were producing for the German military were intended as anti-tank strategy, desperately needed on the front lines at the time.

Adi and Rudolf were a valuable asset to Germany's manufacturing, but even so, the war eventually raged on so long and so hard that even they were called to duty. The brothers were both over the age of 40 at the time. Adi was allowed to return to the factory within a year, so that he could ensure production would continue smoothly. Rudolf wasn't so lucky, he had to remain an active part of the German military regime. It is said that he went on to join the infamous Gestapo, the Nazi secret police, a claim that he would both give credence to, and refute, after the war.

Sibling Rivalry – Two Companies

The stories surrounding why the Dassler brothers had a parting of ways vary greatly and there are a lot of urban legends surrounding the circumstances. The only thing that we know for certain is that the two would part ways in 1948, never to reconcile again. The complications of being in business together, and differences in politics, would drive a wedge between the brothers.

Allied troops began to close in on Germany and eventually, in 1945, the war came to Herzogenaurach. Rudolf wasn't there when Allied bombers targeted their town, but his family was. The sirens began to blare and the bombs were falling, destroying much of the town in the process. The Nazis had subjected England to the same fate, but the tide had begun to turn against them. The Nazis were about to fall and the Dassler family began to fracture and split under the stress and strain of war. The story goes that Adi and his family hid in the basement along with Rudolf's wife and children. One particular time, Adi, Käthe, and their son were the last to find refuge in the shelter. Adi was pacing with a nervous anger, grumbling the phrase, 'back again…the swine'. Friedl was convinced that Adi was referring to her and her children, rather than the Allied forces. It had to be stressful to be without Rudolf during those trying times, so it's not surprising that her mood was heightened. This incident is said to have further soured the already tense relationship between the two families.

Due to their complementing personalities as brothers, Adi had always left a lot of the business up to Rudolf. When Adi married Käthe he found someone with a strong personality, similar to his beloved brother. Unfortunately, Rudolf and Käthe did not get along. Rudolf was often a tyrant to Käthe and the two would constantly experience conflict within the family business.

The Post-War Escape

It was during the aftermath of the fall of Nazi Germany that some of the risky decisions made by the Dassler brothers during the 1936 Olympics would come back to help them. The Second World War was coming to a close and Rudolf could finally return home to Herzogenaurach. The Allied troops were making their way through Germany and the surrounding areas, destroying all of the factories that had been producing instruments of war for the Nazis. The Americans set their sights on Herzogenaurach in April of 1945. The story goes that the troops rolled into town and it was Adi's wife Käthe, whose ingenuity and quick thinking, saved the family business from certain destruction. The story goes that the Americans had pulled their tanks right up to the front of the Dassler Brothers factory and were preparing to destroy the building. Käthe Dassler was a woman with a gentle and kind face. She could also be quite charming and persuasive when the situation called for it and the tense moments that she encountered that fateful day outside of the factory were probably the most urgent of her life. Käthe was somehow able to charm the American soldiers into leaving their factory standing, convincing them that they only produced footwear and weren't a part of the Nazi war machine, which couldn't have been further from the truth.

The close call that the Dassler family experienced wasn't the last of it. Germany was far from a peaceful place in the period following the Second World War. The Allies were busy interrogating anyone who could have been involved with the Nazi regime and were imprisoning citizens in droves.

Eventually, the Americans came to interrogate Adi. Adi also charmed the military interrogators, being sure to punch home the fact that he had equipped American athletes, such as Jesse Owens, at the Olympics. This impressed the Americans and he was released; he was a free man.

It was no longer business as usual for the Dassler brothers, as each brother wanted to be in charge and felt that there was only room for one. They then had to decide who would run the company as it re-established itself in post-war Germany. Rudolf was also interviewed by the Americans about his denazification, but his experience wouldn't go quite as smoothly as Adi. It is important to note that Adi served the Nazi regime in the military for one year, while Rudolf had remained an active member of the Nazis until the end of the war. Rudolf's past as a Nazi was an issue that he had to address to the interrogators and he was quickly in a fight for his factory and his future. He foolishly and boldly declared to his interrogators that he had worked for the Nazi Gestapo, but would later retract his statements. These impulsive actions showed a man frustrated by the devastating German loss in the war. He was clearly more emotionally invested in the war efforts than his brother.

Rudolf was subsequently sent to an American internment camp. It was while he was there that he began to become suspicious about how he had ended up there. An American told him that he had been denounced by someone close to him, and he suspected that Adi and/or his wife Käthe were the originators of a conspiracy. The thought of this enraged him and a lifelong grudge was born. It was a grudge that would change the Dassler family and the shoe industry forever. He had long distrusted his sister-in-law and it wasn't a stretch for him to think that she was behind it all. Rudolf had always found her to be manipulative and desirous of too much control of the company. He had no proof of course, but that didn't matter. He told the Americans that his internment had to be from false accusations and after a year in the camp, Rudolf was finally released and able to return home to Herzogenaurach and his family.

During the time that Rudolf was away, Adi went looking for new business opportunities. He began making baseball and basketball boots for the Americans, which allowed the Dassler Brothers to survive during those difficult post-war repair days. American sports were a major focus of the company for the first time. Adi and his wife had been running everything in Rudolf's absence, while his wife Friedl had to sit by almost powerless, just trying all she could to protect her husband's stake in the company. Adi managed to grow quite a lot as a craftsman and became an expert in modernising sports' gear.

Rudolf returned to a very different landscape at home. The Dassler family villa was requisitioned for use by American soldiers, so the family was now living in the factory tower. The conditions there were close and cramped, which naturally lead to emotional clashes and fighting amongst the two families. The brothers would fight about everything from money to control. The breaking point came when Adi was interrogated for an unprecedented second time by the Americans. Coming so long after he had already been cleared, it was obvious that someone had tipped-off the authorities to issues with Adi's denazification. Rudolf had tried to discredit his brother, badmouthing him to the authorities. The Americans would soon drop the case against Adi, seeing quickly that it was one disgruntled brother's word against another.

It was impossible to run a business together after all the post-war drama so, in 1948, the Dassler brothers decided that they had to divide the company in half. The workforce was quickly notified and the separation began. Rudolf assembled all of the employees to tell them that the brothers were forming two different companies and that they would all need to choose which brother to follow, because once they left with one brother, they wouldn't be welcome to work for the other. It is estimated that about two thirds of the workforce sided with Adi, which primarily consisted of the shoemakers, while most of the salesmen went with Rudolf.

The news shocked the workers and naturally rumours began to swirl about the real reason for the split. The most prevalent were rumours of an affair between Rudolf and his sister-in-law. The employees had a major decision to make: did they follow the salesman or the inventor? The brothers divided up the materials and machinery and set up competing shoe manufacturing businesses a mere 500m apart from each other. Adi started 'Adidas' and Rudolf founded 'Puma'. The local population eventually got drawn into the conflict. The companies each had their own football club and the two teams were bitter rivals. Puma and Adidas employees wouldn't even sit at the same table while drinking at their local pub. It's hard to say whether the divide was due to extreme loyalty, or fear of being associated with the enemy and being fired.

The two brothers and their families never made-up and their bitter feud lasted until the time of their deaths. The two companies did issue a press release in 2009 to announce that Adidas and Puma would come together to participate in their first joint activity since the two companies opened back in 1948. They united to support the Peace One Day organisation for its annual non-violence day.

Chapter Five

Chanel: Hitler's Seductive Spy

You know, they ask me questions. Just an example: 'What do you wear to bed?
A pajama top? The bottoms of the pajamas? A nightgown?' So I said,
'Chanel No. 5,' because it's the truth… And yet, I don't want to say 'nude.'
But it's the truth!

— Marilyn Monroe

The name Coco Chanel is synonymous with fashion and haute couture. The enduring brand name has survived and thrived long after the passing of its namesake. Chanel has been regarded by some as the greatest fashion designer who ever lived, she is certainly one of the most infamous. Her name has endured, not only on clothing, but also jewellery, handbags and of course perfume. Her magnum opus, Chanel No. 5, is one of the most popular and best-selling fragrances of all-time. Coco was a powerful and ambitious businesswoman and a pioneer in many ways. She was also widely regarded as a vicious and horrible person, a Nazi sympathiser, and eventually even a Nazi spy.

Her Early Life

Gabrielle 'Coco' Chanel had a troubled early life. She was born on 19 August 1883 in Saumur, Maine-et-Loire, France. Chanel was, literally, born in the poorhouse, specifically the Sisters of Providence charity hospital. Her mother, Eugenie Jeanne Devolle, worked in the poorhouse as a laundrywoman, and her father, Albert Chanel, was a travelling street vendor. The level of poverty that Gabrielle was born into should not be underplayed, and in fact played a large part in shaping her character throughout her life.

The French commune into which Chanel was born was very similar to a municipality in America. Saumur was a self-governed and somewhat isolated town tucked snugly between the Loire and Thouet rivers and surrounded by vineyards. The commune is located near the famous Champagne wine region and was well known for its sparkling wines. The Saumur area has been settled for thousands of years in one form or another. The ornate skyline of the town includes the impressive Chateau de Saumur castle that was constructed as a stronghold to protect the region from the advancing Normans in the tenth century. The chateau was sacked and later rebuilt by King Henry II. The town later served as a state prison under the rule of Napoleon and is famous for being the base of operations for the French military riding academy, and for its wine. During the Second World War, the German forces advanced on the town in an attempt to head-off the newly landed Allied forces in Normandy; the town was badly damaged from bombings and the German Panzer tanks rumbling through the area. Saumur would be awarded the Croix de Guerre after the war in tribute to the resistance and patriotism demonstrated by the townspeople in the face of great danger.

Saumur may have been an ornate and beautiful area, but the reality of life was very different for those in the lower classes. The sweeping poor laws of the previous century had produced exploitative and harsh workhouses, also known as poorhouses, in an effort to provide accommodation and provisions for the poor. The workhouse wasn't a pleasant place for a child to grow-up. If you weren't a highborn individual, then you could look forward to a life of poverty and hard work. The able-bodied women were put to work doing a variety of domestic jobs like sewing, cleaning, cooking, gardening or laundry. Gabrielle's mother worked as a laundrywoman for the charity hospital run by the Sisters of Providence.

Life in the poorhouse was a difficult one. The toilet facilities in the workhouses were used by well over one hundred inmates and would also often include a communal chamber pot. The men and women were kept separate to avoid indiscretions. The children would also often be housed separately, at least when it came to sleeping quarters, and were subject to bed sharing to save space. The pre-set diet in the workhouse consisted primarily of bread, gruel and cheese. If you were lucky you might get a small serving of meat up to twice a week. The set restrictions could provide, for example, a meagre supper that included 5oz of bread and 1.5oz of cheese for an adult woman. The children in the workhouse were typically afforded the same diet as an adult woman, as long as they were over the age of 9; if you were under 9 it was up to the discretion of the staff. Meals were eaten in a large communal hall that often included the reading of biblical texts out loud to remind the inmates of the gratitude that they should be feeling for the charity that was being bestowed upon them.

Chanel would find herself in an orphanage by the time she was 12 years old. Her mother had died of bronchitis and her father had sent her and her two sisters away to live at the convent of Aubazine, where she would remain until the age of 18. Her time with the nuns in the convent would provide her with the groundwork that would come to build her entire empire – and change her fate forever – the ability to sew. This loss at a young age and lack of familial attachment would help mould her into an independent person who had little conflict putting her own needs first.

Coco Chanel faced a special amount of difficulty as a woman in French society. We all know that life was far more difficult for women in the late nineteenth and early twentieth centuries, but the role of a woman in French culture was especially bleak, especially if you had any ambitions outside of marriage and motherhood. French women wouldn't even gain their right to vote until the tail end of the Second World War, the first election that allowed women to vote in France was on 29 April 1945. It was only under the Provincial French Committee of National Liberation, headed by now legendary General Charles de Gaulle, that the right was provided to the women of France. French society has been isolationist over the years and the rights and roles of women in politics and society alike have grown at a slower pace than similarly developed nations. Germany, by contrast, has allowed women to vote since 1918, and America since 1920. The suffragette movement encountered a great deal of difficulty in piercing the thick, misogynistic cloud that loomed over French culture.

It wasn't uncommon in French culture at the time for married men to live a nomadic and unreliable lifestyle, often travelling for work and leaving their families back at home. The duties of caring for the children, the home, and often even working on the side to help support the family, would fall upon the shoulders of the woman. Life in France was so laced with misogyny that it wasn't until 1965 that a married woman could obtain the right to work without her husband's consent. In the case of Gabrielle Chanel, her mother was an unmarried woman who lived with Gabrielle and her four siblings in a workhouse. A paradox of Victorian France is that an unmarried woman would be granted more rights than a married one. A single woman could own property and pay her own taxes to the state; she had more advantages and opportunities than a married woman, though even then they were limited by society. Albert did eventually marry Chanel's mother, but only after her family paid him to do so.

When Chanel's mother died, the reality faced by the children was bleak, at best. A girl of only 12, Gabrielle was at a tender age to lose her mother. The existence she had faced with her mother alive was destined to be difficult enough, but to lose her had to be devastating to her young psyche. This was likely only compounded by the actions of her father, Albert. A travelling street vendor wasn't about to take on the task of raising five children. Gabrielle's brothers were given to a peasant family and she, along with her two sisters, were brought to the convent in Aubazine by their father and abandoned. It was this harsh and painful action that would shape Gabrielle and her future, changing her fate forever.

The only hope that Gabrielle had to become the designer and woman that she truly wanted to be was to remain free, and to remain free in France she would have to stay single. This fact presented her with a new problem: it wasn't easy for a woman to gain funding or support for opening her own business, so she would have to rely on private funding.

Gabrielle eventually began a small singing career in French nightclubs, where she went by the moniker 'Coco'. There is a lot of misinformation out there about the life of Coco Chanel, most of which was spread by Coco herself. Over time, she was found to have provided several conflicting stories about her childhood and early life to various reporters and friends. For example, she once told editor-in-chief of *Marie-Claire,* Marcel Haedrich, that the origins of her nickname were from her father. 'My father used to call me 'Little Coco' until something better should come along. He didn't like 'Gabrielle' at all; it hadn't been his choice.' In an interview with *The Atlantic* however, Gabrielle claimed that her nickname was a shortened version of the French term coquette, which refers to a kept woman, or a woman of loose morals. Although, it has been noted that during her time as a singer in the La Rotunde club in Vichy she sang the songs 'Ko Ko Ri Ko' and 'Who's seen Coco in the Trocadero?'

Coco wasn't shy about her sexuality and took many lovers throughout her lifetime. The life of a cabaret singer wasn't exactly the culmination of a dream for Coco and she soon found herself a kept woman, the coquette lover of Etienne Balsan, a handsome young French socialite and the son of wealthy industrialists providing uniforms to the military. Chanel was just one of Balsan's mistresses, but this wasn't an uncommon part of French upper crust society.

Balsan would assist Chanel in opening her first boutique selling hats and dresses, a venture to keep her occupied while he was away tending to other interests. Balsan also introduced Chanel to Arthur 'Boy' Capel, who would soon become another of Chanel's lovers. Coming from a financially troubled background, Chanel was intoxicated by what the cultural tradition of being a mistress could provide her with. The entire affair was often treated more like a business transaction than a passionate love affair, a stipulation that fit Chanel's personality quite well. Coco could quite possibly have lived out her life in comfort jumping from lover to lover, but she had her own ideas about her journey. Coco would use the financial benefits of her relationships to launch her own fashion empire.

The Beginnings of an Empire

In 1910 Chanel opened her very first boutique at 21 Rue Cambon in Paris, designing lavish hats. The simple elegance of her aesthetic soon swept through Paris. Chanel moved on to opening more boutique-style stores, including one in Deauville in 1913. There she introduced her line of sportswear, something that would revolutionise how women dressed and create an entire genre of clothing that is more popular today than ever. In 1915 Chanel made the biggest move of her career up to that point: banking on the reputation she had built over the previous five years, she opened her first couture House in Biarritz followed by the now famous Chanel Fashion House at 31 Rue Cambon in Paris in 1918.

On 5 May 1921, Chanel made possibly her biggest lasting mark on the world: she introduced the fragrance Chanel No5. The scent was created by Ernest Beaux and was given its name simply because it was the fifth fragrance presented to Chanel. Coco would unveil other fragrances in her lifetime, but none so timeless as Chanel No. 5. The purpose of the fragrance was to create a unique scent to epitomise the flapper and the revolutionary spirit of the 1920s.

The 1920s was a time of change and revolution, especially in the United States. The post-war decade began with the prohibition of alcohol and women finally being given the right to vote, a right that had been granted to women over the age of 30 two years earlier in England (the right to vote was finally granted to all women aged 21 and over in 1928). It is now a well-known fact that the act of prohibition didn't stop people drinking alcohol; in fact it simply gave rise to organised crime. The United States was littered with seedy nightclubs and speakeasies run by questionable types that would offer alcohol on the sly. These establishments became a huge part of culture throughout the 1920s, especially for the younger crowd. Along with these clubs came the new and hip sound of Jazz music; coupled with a burgeoning fashion scene and rapid economic growth, the decade grew into what we refer to now as the Roaring Twenties.

The movement of women's fashion throughout the 1920s was towards dropping the often restrictive and punishing corsets and petticoats of past centuries in favour of a comfortable fashion; a trend that would change not only fashion, but also the way women were perceived in culture. The first major clothing revolution that Coco Chanel would mastermind could be referred to as 'La Garconne', which is French for 'Boyish'. This would be used to describe what is known in America as the 'Flapper' fashion movement, a style that would come to define the look of the period. During the mid-1920s Coco unveiled one of her most enduring fashion contributions: the little black dress. Being responsible for some of these wildly successful fashion revolutions would be enough of a résumé to keep the Chanel name in the history books, but Coco was never one to rest on her laurels.

In 1924, Coco wanted to expand the customer base for her Chanel No. 5 fragrance, but a move that grand required some serious financing. The Parfums Chanel corporate entity was created with backing from the well-to-do, Jewish, Wertheimer family. I note that they were a Jewish family for reasons that will become integral later in this chapter. The deal wasn't even slightly in Chanel's benefit, giving a seventy per cent stake in the company to the Wertheimers and only ten per cent of the stock to Coco for the licensing of her name. The remaining twenty per cent was awarded to Theophile Bader, who was instrumental in brokering the deal. The entire experience left Coco Chanel bitter.

The Successful Monster

Chanel would find more glamour in her life when she was called out to Hollywood to design for the stars in 1931, at the direct invitation of famed silver-screen studio head, Samuel Goldwyn. Quickly becoming a fashion legend and a legitimate member of the 'in' crowd, Coco revelled in her newfound American fame. She befriended various posh celebrities of the era such as Russian composer Igor Stravinsky and artist Pablo Picasso. Chanel would reach the peak of her fame and reputation in the 1930s, and by 1935 she was running five boutiques on Rue Cambon in Paris and was employing over 4,000 workers.

When the Second World War reached Paris, Chanel actually closed four of her boutiques, leaving many women out of work. A number of her biographers suggest that this move was done in retaliation to a labour dispute she had had with her workers a few years before, and that the opportunity to put them out of work was a vindictive action. The shop at 31 Rue Cambon remained open, often frequented by American soldiers looking to obtain gifts to send to their sweethearts back home. Little did these brave men know that the head of the House of Chanel was working for the enemy.

It is often echoed in biographies and articles that Coco Chanel was a horrible woman, a monster even; a sentiment that has been presented time and again from various sources. There is no doubt that her association with the Nazis was heinous, but this reputation came long before those revelations began to become public over a decade ago. One has to wonder how much of Coco's poor reputation has to do with her being savvy and a strong businesswoman who took no prisoners and would not accept defeat? Would a man be given the same labels, or would he be labelled 'industrious' and 'strong'? Her beginnings, born into a workhouse and abandoned in her early adolescence, made Chanel strong and determined. It is certainly a strength that should be admired, even if her actions shouldn't always have been.

The Nazi Occupation of France

It was during the Nazi occupation of Paris that Coco Chanel would embark on a path that was to leave her name forever tarnished. It was in the early years of the Second World War that Hitler set his sights on the spoils and glamour of France. The German forces, complete with planes and tanks, rolled into France in May of 1940. The Fall of France was a brief affair; the French forces were defeated and surrendered in just six weeks. It was a humbling and even humiliating experience for the French; after all, they boasted the second most powerful military in Europe at the time. The reputation for military excellence came for the French during the First World War.

Once France had fallen, the French signed a surrender armistice with Germany that, in simplified form, split France into an occupied and an unoccupied zone. The northern part of France, including Paris, would be occupied by the Nazi regime. The Nazi occupying forces would set up a puppet government, referred to as the Vichy regime. This anti-Semitic French governing system was established to control the region more easily. Vichy was an area in France that, in the pre-war era, was a holiday destination known for its spas and refreshing water. The Nazis also moved into Vichy, along with the new French government officials. There was a serious need for space, so they moved into the various hotels in the city, kicking out the tourists. The head of the Vichy regime was French First World War hero Marshal Phillipe Pétain. The aged war hero would soon fall prey to the influence and menace of the Nazi propaganda machine.

On Thursday, 24 October 1940, French President Pétain and his Vice President Pierre Laval, met with Adolf Hitler in the isolated commune of Montoire. Hitler came to the meeting with Dr Paul Schmidt, his translator, and his Foreign Minister, Joachim von Ribbentrop. The aim of Pétain was to negotiate the armistice with Germany and end their mutual hostilities for the good of his country. His actions that day, and the infamous photograph of him shaking hands with Adolf Hitler, would call his loyalty to France into question in the coming years and he is sometimes regarded as a collaborator. In reality, by working with the Nazis instead of against them, he was doing what he believed to be right. He agreed to peace, but refused to join the Nazi war machine. On 30 October 1940, Pétain addressed the French people in a speech titled 'Cette Collaboration diot être sincère', which revealed to the people that he had met with Hitler and had every intention of working with the Nazis and meeting their terms.

President Pétain had the trust of the French people, but his speech left them confused and uncertain about what was happening. The French expected more resistance and instead they got compromise. There was a certain level of resistance and the desire to resist the Nazi regime by the French people, but there was very little that the average citizen could actually do. The best that most could manage was the silent resistance of keeping their lives as normal as possible and refusing to acknowledge or accept the Nazi occupation of France, a move that has come under heavy criticism over the years. Silence of resistance, or silence of complacency? On the other hand, resistance could easily mean death.

Adolf Hitler travelled to Paris only once during the war, with Albert Speer his Minister of Armaments and War Production, and entourage of various other Nazis. The Fuhrer visited the Eiffel Tower and Arc de Carrousel as a tourist on 28 June 1940. Hitler may not have remained in Paris, or even France, but the Nazi soldiers did. They occupied the streets of Paris with a menacing and foreboding presence.

On 20 June 1942 the Nazis began to require every Jew in France to sew a patch of the Star of David, whether they were French or foreign. If you were not wearing the star and were suspected to be a Jewish man on the streets, you could be stopped and questioned and even suffer the indignity of being forced to pull your pants down to prove the point, to extreme humiliation and embarrassment. It is an ancient tradition for Jewish males to be circumcised, a practice not commonly seen at the time in Europe. The Jews in France were eventually rounded-up and deported to concentration camps. The single largest round up of Jewish people during the occupation of France took place on 16 July 1942; approximately 15,000 Jews, many of whom were women and children, were rounded up by the French police and placed in a sport's stadium for a week without food, water or sanitation.

A good number of people died from thirst and malnutrition. The Jews from this roundup were eventually transferred to Auchwitz, never to be seen or heard from again.

Control of Chanel No. 5 removed from Jewish Owners

The deal that brokered Parfums Chanel left Coco bitter and her ego bruised, not to mention her pocketbook. The company was a goldmine from which she was unable to adequately profit. Chanel lamented her decision, 'I signed something in 1924. I let myself be swindled.' Those around Chanel advised her that all was well with the profits that she was enjoying, but Chanel was convinced that she was being taken for a fool. She didn't care to take into account the amount of financial investment that it took to bring Chanel No.5 into the worldwide marketplace. Chanel would hire attorney Rene de Chambrun, a suspected Nazi collaborator, to begin various lawsuits against the Wertheimers in 1930. Over the years her various suits were wildly unsuccessful and it wasn't until the Nazi occupation of France that she would get her first viable opportunity. The desire to gain control of the company bearing her namesake, and a relatively loose moral fibre, instigated Chanel to take advantage of the Nazi aryanisation of all Jewish-owned businesses.

The Nazi party had clearly laid out their intentions in their original twenty-five-point ideology over two decades before Chanel would get involved with the party. The intention of full segregation of Jews from their Aryan society was well underway in 1941, and had been since the Nuremberg Laws were passed in 1935. It took less than a year for two thirds of all Jewish-owned businesses in Germany to be transferred to non-Jewish Germans at a price that was well below the market value. Also, all Jewish managers and employees were fired. The ability for anyone of Jewish descent to make a living was effectively removed from Germany – and for any region that the Nazis would conquer. This would eventually include France.

When France fell in May and June of 1940, it was an enormous blow to the collective psyche of the European people who still had hope of resisting the dark shadow being cast by Hitler. The imagery of Hitler and the Nazis rolling into Paris and gleefully enjoying the sights, like the Eiffel Tower, are still to this day a vivid and haunting snapshot into what could have easily been the fate of the rest of Europe, and perhaps the world. Once France had fallen to the Nazis, it took Chanel only a year to devise a plan that would live in infamy.

On 5 May 1941 Coco Chanel wrote the following in a letter to the Nazi party, stating her case for the return of Parfums Chanel to her full ownership:

> *Parfums Chanel is still the property of Jews … and has been legally 'abandoned' by the owners. I have an indisputable right of priority. The profits that I have received from my creations since the foundation of this business…are disproportionate.*

There is little doubt that the plan would have worked just the way she had wanted, but Chanel hadn't accounted for the planning and cunning of the wealthy. It turned out that the Jewish man who owned that controlling stake in Parfums Chanel, Pierre Wertheimer, had foreseen the Nazi movement across Europe and had fled to New York to avoid the inevitable persecution. It was his actions prior to fleeing that Chanel did not anticipate. Wertheimer transferred the ownership of Parfums Chanel over to Felix Amiot before he left. Amiot was a French businessman without a drop of Jewish blood in his family line. This move is likely all that kept the company out of the clutches of Chanel during the war. Amiot turned the company back over to Wertheimer's control once the war was over.

The 1924 contract to gain Parfums Chanel was again an issue when Coco had the nerve to bring the case up again, this time post-war in a court of law.

The Nazi Mistress

When Adolf Hitler became the German Chancellor in 1933, the rise to power for the Nazi leader was soon in full swing and he would soon make a carefully crafted move to full dictatorship. The regime of the Third Reich involved many branches, from the Luftwaffe (German Air Force) to the Schutzstaffel (SS) and the German secret police, Geheime Staatspolizei (Gestapo). These were the well-known divisions of the Nazis, but there were several departments, including a propaganda wing called Public Enlightenment and Propaganda, and the Abwehr. The Abwehr was a secret German military intelligence organisation that had been established in 1920. In the post-First World War era, Germany wasn't allowed to engage in any espionage, thanks to the Treaty of Versailles, an agreement that would also levy harsh restrictions on the country.

When Hitler took power he gained control of the Abwehr and in 1938 he organised the branch into a more effective intelligence-gathering unit. It was Joseph Goebbels himself, the Reich Minister for Public Enlightenment

John Sith Pemberton portrait (Author unknown, Source: Creative Commons).

Vintage Coca-Cola advertisement.

Vintage Coca-Cola advertisement (c. 1911).

SA.-, SS.-, HJ.-Uniformen

Arbeits-, Sport- u. Regenkleidung

aus eigener Herstellung in bekannt guten Qualitäten und billigen Preisen

BOSS

Mech. Berufskleiderfabrik, Metzingen

Zugelassene Lieferfirma für SA. und SS. Uniformen der Reichszeugmeisterei München unter Nr. 53

Hugo Boss company newspaper advertisement (date unknown).

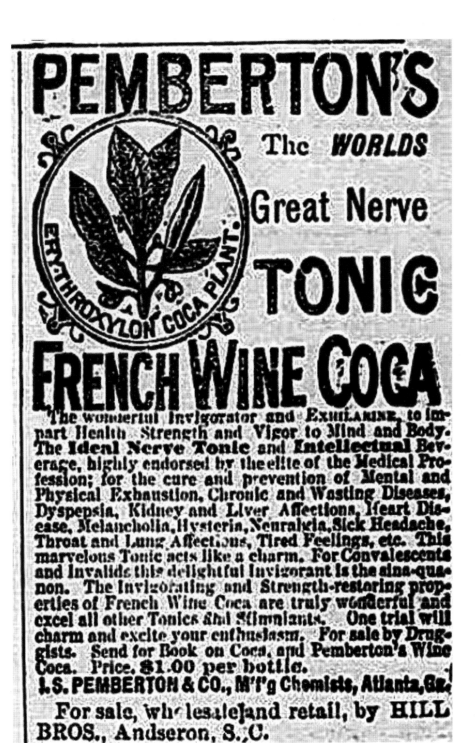

Pemberton's French Wine Coca newspaper advertisement.

Henry Ford Portrait (c. 1919, Hartsook, photographer. Source: Library of Congress).

Henry Ford with the ten millionth Model T (Source: Library of Congress).

The Ford International Weekly
THE DEARBORN
INDEPENDENT

One Dollar   Dearborn, Michigan, May 22, 1920   Five Cents

The International Jew:
The World's Problem

"Among the distinguishing mental and moral traits of the Jews may be mentioned: distaste
for hard or violent physical labor; a strong family sense and philoprogenitiveness; a marked

The Dearborn Independent newspaper (1920).

'Jesse Owens at start of record breaking 200 meter race' (1936, Source: Library of Congress).

Hugo F. Boss's Nazi membership (c. 1931).

The Dassler shoe factory (Source: Library of Congress).

Coco Chanel portrait (c. 1910, Source: Library of Congress).

'Der Führer in Paris' Adolf Hitler visiting occupied Paris, France (c. 1940, Source: The National Archives).

Ford Factory assembly line (c. 1913, Source: Library of Congress).

BAYER Pharmaceutical Products
HEROIN—HYDROCHLORIDE

is pre-eminently adapted for the manufacture
of cough elixirs, cough balsams, cough drops,
cough lozenges, and cough medicines of any
kind.   Price in 1 oz. packages, $4.85 per
ounce ; less in larger quantities.   The efficient dose being very small (1-48 to 1-24 gr.),
it is

The Cheapest Specific for the Relief of Coughs
(In bronchitis, phthisis, whooping cough, etc., etc.)

WRITE FOR LITERATURE TO

FARBENFABRIKEN OF ELBERFELD COMPANY
SELLING AGENTS

P. O. Box 2160   40 Stone Street, NEW YORK

Bayer heroin newspaper
advertisement (c. 1901).

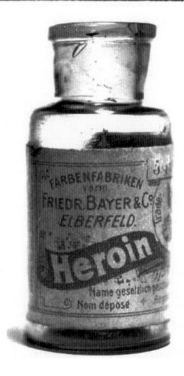

Bayer & Co. bottle of heroin.

Entrance to the German death camp Auschwitz, in Poland (Logaritmo, Photographer, Source: Creative Commons).

John Harvey Kellogg portrait (c. 1914, Source: Library of Congress).

A STEADY CUSTOMER

Healthy children, if allowed to follow their appetites, are steady customers for Kellogg's Toasted Corn Flakes.

Winter or summer it's their favorite food.

More than a million American families eat Kellogg's the year around.

To get the original toasted corn flakes—the quality kind with the Waxtite package protection—ask your grocer for KELLOGG'S and look for this signature:

Vintage Kellogg's cereal advertisement (c. 1915, Source: Library of Congress).

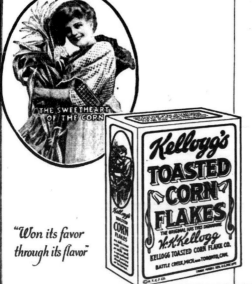

Vintage Kellogg's cereal advertisement (c. 1919, Source: Library of Congress).

Workers outside of the Winchester Repeating Arms Company
(c. 1897, Source: Library of Congress).

The Winchester mansion (c. 1980, HABS, photographer, Source: Library of Congress).

Sarah Winchester's bedroom (c. 1980, HABS, photographer, Source: Library of Congress).

The Winchester mansion living room fireplace (c. 1980, HABS, photographer, Source: Library of Congress).

Leo Baekeland portrait (c. 1906, Source: Library of Congress).

Bakelite laboratory in Younkers, NY (c. 1935, Source: Bakelite Review/ Library of Congress).

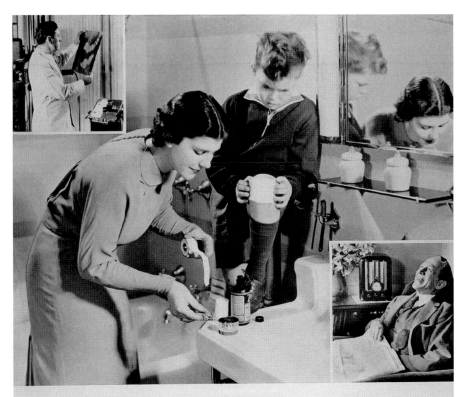

HELPING THE FAMILY KEEP WELL . . . .

WHEN a venturesome youngster stumbles and cuts his knee, his mother never thinks of bandaging it with strips of old linen. She cleanses the cut with an antiseptic, and bandages it with gauze and a moisture-proof, germ-proof adhesive plaster. In this simple emergency doctoring she has been aided by two Bakelite Materials. One type is used for the bottle closure that protects the purity of the antiseptic. The other is a flexible resinoid that moisture-proofs the adhesive plaster.

When you visit the doctor for your annual health inventory, Bakelite materials again come into service. Examination of your throat is conducted with an ora-light produced from Bakelite Molded. More perfect X-Ray photographs of vital organs are obtained with greater certainty because of the Bakelite materials which have been used throughout the X-Ray machine, from the insulation for the current conducting parts to the switches, wheels and regulators that are used to operate the equipment.

When the dentist advises a dental restoration, it no longer need cause great concern, for the appearance of healthy oral tissue is now closely simulated by LUXENE

resinoid, a translucent pink denture material developed to assure the utmost in natural appearance and comfort.

Even the deaf are benefited by hearing aids with amplifiers and ear pieces produced from lustrous black Bakelite Molded. The elderly and infirm, and shut-ins everywhere, are able to keep in touch with the world through the medium of radio, which utilizes Bakelite materials throughout its entire construction, including the rich, lustrous molded cabinet.

These are a few of the scores of ways in which Bakelite Materials, products of creative chemical research, are aiding physicians and surgeons, dentists and oculists in promoting the health and comfort of all.

Bakelite Corporation, 247 Park Avenue, New York, N.Y.
Bakelite Corporation of Canada, Ltd., 163 Dufferin St., Toronto

Particularly for Manufacturers

•

All major industries are making profitable use of one or more Bakelite Materials, either through using them in the product itself, in production machinery, or in maintenance.

•

Some forms are used in every branch of the electrical industry, others in the process industries, and still others in the mechanical industries. Pharmaceutical, cosmetic, food, and liquor industries use Bakelite Materials for containers, closures and merchandise displays. The building industry uses them for decorative effects both indoors and out. Furniture, hardware, paint and varnish, textile, and automotive are other industries making wide use of them.

•

We urge you to look into the possibilities of Bakelite Materials for your own business. Our engineers will be glad to advise you. As a first step we invite you to write for our illustrated booklets "Bakelite Molded" 27M, "Bakelite Laminated" 27L and "Bakelite Varnish" 27V.

BAKELITE

The registered trade mark shown above distinguish materials manufactured by Bakelite Corporation. Under the capital "B" in the hexagon symbol of present and future uses of Bakelite Corporation's products.

The Material Of a Thousand Uses

Vintage Bakelite magazine advertisement (Source: Library of Congress).

Bakelite jewellery colours (c. 1924, Source: Gifts to Treasure, Embed Art Company catalogue).

and Propaganda, who would appoint Abwehr spy Baron Hans Gunther von Dincklage to the position of 'special attaché' to the German Embassy in Paris in 1933. The position that Dincklage held should not be underestimated. His German Embassy position provided him with the extremely convenient and effective veil of diplomatic immunity to work and plot while in France. His actions didn't fall beneath the notice of the French intelligence community. Records reveal that they had been watching Dincklage since 1919. The French knew full well that he was a German Abwehr agent and even that his agent identification code was F-8680.

Once Dincklage got his attaché position he was able to move into a wealthy area of Paris and could be seen sporting around town in his flashy grey Chrysler roadster. Even his live-in maid, Lucie Braun, was a Nazi agent. The primary purpose of having the Baron as the attaché was to allow him the ability to gather intelligence effectively by planting employees in various key places, like factories and various government agencies. In 1934 the Abwehr agents were directed by the Nazi hierarchy to work more closely with the Gestapo to organise and execute espionage. It was, in fact, the very first Nazi cell in France.

Chanel had moved to a gorgeous suite in the famed Hotel Ritz, Paris. The high ceilings and ornate but elegant style made it the place to be if you had means. To this day, the Ritz has a famed reputation for its lavish atmosphere and unique culinary experience. Cesar Ritz opened the hotel bearing his name right on the place Vendome, a square that sits at the start of the Rue de la Paix, a fashionable shopping district. Ritz promised that his hotel would offer 'all the refinements that a Prince might hope to find in his own private residence'. It's said that his own investors complimented Cesar on his hotel at the opening, proclaiming: 'Kings and Princes will be envious of you, Ritz. You're going to teach the world how one should live.' The move to the Ritz was no small hallmark in the life of Chanel, a woman who came from meagre beginnings. Her apartment there was, literally, the lap of luxury and high society.

During this time she was seeing designer Paul Iribe, who worked with *Vogue* magazine doing illustrations and design. The relationship between Iribe and Chanel started in 1931. Iribe, like all good artists, had his muse. The two would collaborate on a provocative magazine, titled *Le Témoin*, Iribe as illustrator and Chanel as financier. *Le Témoin* was well known as a purveyor of anti-Semitism and aggressive nationalism. The heroine of the illustrations within was Marianne, a symbol of French liberty. Iribe clearly modelled Marianne after Chanel herself. Chanel was deeply in love with

Iribe and the two looked likely to wed, but in 1935, during a rousing game of tennis, Iribe collapsed and died in front of Chanel. She was devastated by the loss. Chanel mourned, but continued to move forward with her work, unaware that the world was about to be plunged into war.

Chanel and the French authorities were well aware of Dincklage's Nazi connections and his work as an agent of espionage. During the pre-war era his dealings were revealed by French counter-intelligence agents and were published in the newspaper *Vendémiaire*. There was no denying knowledge of his exploits, so when Chanel embarked upon a relationship with the Baron, she knew full well who she was getting into bed with. The moment that Coco and Hans met is not known; Coco would tell officials after the war that she had known him for decades, while others place their meeting sometime in the 1930s. Regardless of the truth, by the time the Nazis had taken France, the Hotel Ritz where Chanel resided had become a reserved place for senior Nazi officials. Chanel was one of the few foreigners who was allowed to remain.

Paris had fallen and refugees had fled to the South. There was Nazi propaganda at every street corner, signs and posters served as an ominous reminder to citizens that obedience to the new occupying forces would be in their best interest. Chanel was 57 when she and Dincklage became lovers in 1940. Hans was a cultured, pleasant and handsome man and a great conquest for Chanel in the newly occupied Paris. It was Dincklage who would facilitate all of the Nazi dealings that Chanel would have during the war. It is assumed that it must have been her connection with Dincklage that allowed Chanel to remain at the Ritz, where only a chosen few non-Germans were permitted to remain in residence. Only a handful of known Nazi collaborators and the wife of the hotel founder were allowed to stay, along with Coco Chanel. The times would soon become hard for French citizens, with many families facing starvation. All the while, the German officials, including Dincklage and Chanel, would dine lavishly in the well-guarded confines of the Ritz. In much the same way that the eight-man band continued to play their cheerful songs for the aristocracy while the RMS *Titanic* sunk around them, the high society of Paris continued on their typical merry way, while Europe came crashing down under the pressures of wartime.

Coco Chanel may not have been regarded as the kindest person in the world and she was certainly a savvy opportunist to take advantage of the Nazi mandates, but that's a far cry from making her a Nazi sympathiser, and certainly far away from any evidence that she was a Nazi spy. There had been whispers and rumours for decades about Chanel's shady dealings throughout the Second World War, and certainly many suspected her involvement, but it wasn't until recently that actual documented proof began to emerge when declassified French intelligence documents were discovered. These documents detailed not only an involvement with the Nazis, but her ascension into actual Nazi spy and the special secret mission that was crafted especially for her.

In 2016, Historians poring over hundreds of boxes of declassified government documents that had been provided to the French Defence Ministry's archives back in 1999, discovered documents that proved the French secret services had suspicions about the extent of Chanel's Nazi connections. These documents, now available to the public (but only in person), reveal a file on Coco Chanel that French intelligence had amongst their files on various celebrities whom they suspected of being Nazi sympathisers. One such document, from 1944, states that: 'A source from Madrid informs us that Madame Chanel, in 1942–1943, was the mistress and agent of Baron Gunther Von Dincklage. Dincklage was the attaché to the German Embassy in Paris in 1935. He worked as a propagandist and was a suspected agent' (translated from the original French).

A French television documentary titled *L'Ombre D'un Doute - Paris and Les Artistes sous l'Occupation*, which aired in late 2014 on France 3, provided further evidence as to the extent of Chanel's involvement with the Nazi regime. Chanel was so involved with the Nazis that she wasn't just dating a spy – she was one herself. Coco went by the code name 'Westminster', which was a reference to her previous relationship with the Duke of Westminster. Her Abwehr involvement was so deep that she was even assigned an agent number, F-7124, according to an official Nazi record. The records of this information were also uncovered in the archives at the French Ministry of Defence.

The idea that Coco Chanel was a Nazi sympathiser, and even a Nazi spy, has only surfaced in recent years, thanks to the declassified French intelligence documents. Coco was, quite literally, sleeping with the enemy. There is an assumption to be made that when someone aligned themselves with the Nazis, they were automatically an anti-Semite. It is easy to jump to that conclusion, but in the case of Coco Chanel I found it difficult to find any evidence that she harboured any particular ill will towards Jews. Coco Chanel may indeed have hated the Jews, and certainly many of her biographers assert this as a fact, but I am reluctant to label anyone without actual proof – or at least a direct quote or two. Obviously, she was no fan of the Jewish family who financed her Parfums Chanel Company, but beyond that I could find no quotes from Chanel to corroborate her being anti-Semitic. Chanel was a cunning opportunist through and through and her work with the Nazis may have been more about the opportunities and advancement it could provide her with over any political or social agenda.

Chanel was the subject of a covert Nazi mission in 1943 by the name of Modellhut ('model hat'). This mission was planned for some time and apparently involved Chanel first travelling to Germany to have a personal meeting with infamous Nazi Heinrich Himmler to plan the details of the mission. We may not be privy to all of the duties that Chanel might have filled as an agent to the Nazis, but we do know about this one key mission, which took place in Madrid (as referenced in the document mentioned above). She travelled to Madrid in 1943 with Hans, with the mission of using her past acquaintanceship with Winston Churchill to persuade him to a ceasefire with Germany through a personal letter, with the hopes of ending the aggressions between England and Germany. In a flurry of arrogance, Chanel was convinced that Churchill would listen to her as a voice of reason. Churchill didn't see it the same way and the deal was ignored.

Chanel was sent on this rather odd mission, because the reality was that Hitler didn't have a mind to continue using his resources in a war with England, but would rather prefer they concede and allow the Nazis to further pursue their intended target: Stalin and the Soviet Union. Reportedly, Hitler even sent his number two, Rudolf Hess, into Britain in 1941 with an offer of peace. Churchill likely refused these ploys for a number of reasons, partly because he knew Hitler wasn't to be trusted and there were no guarantees that the sights of the Nazis wouldn't simply be turned right back on England when they were done with the Soviets.

The documentary series also claims that the post-war records about the involvement of Coco Chanel, and other French celebrities, with the Nazis was scrubbed from existence to preserve the pride of the French resistance and keep from demoralising the public and further tarnishing the spirit of the French people.

The Post-war Getaway

Once the Second World War finally came to a close and the Axis powers were defeated, it was time to rebuild Europe, mourn the losses and hold those still alive accountable for their vast and devastating war crimes. The Nuremberg trials were the world's answer to justice and retribution for the Nazis and their cohorts. Throughout 1945 and 1946 the military tribunals were charged with prosecuting twenty-four members of the remaining Third Reich leadership. One person that was missing from any trials was, of course, Coco Chanel. Well, of course she was missing if the documents that detail her partnership with the Nazis were only recently uncovered, you say? Unfortunately, those documents were classified by the French. The French government took measures to erase the history of Chanel's involvement with the German occupying forces in Paris.

French women who slept with, had relationships with, or were even so much as friendly with German soldiers were accused of 'collaboration horizontale'. In 1944 approximately 35,000 women had their heads shaved by hoards of male French citizens. They were utterly humiliated, stripped naked, and sometimes even had swastikas painted on their bodies. A fate that Coco Chanel craftily avoided. The irony is that many German women suffered the same fate when they cavorted with the French troops as they invaded the Rhineland in 1923. The Nazi party would also make the shaving of women's heads a public punishment for being involved with a non-Aryan. These outbursts of public shaming and humiliation weren't condoned by everyone and many found them to be disgusting displays of misplaced anger or jealousy. The sad reality for many women during the occupation of France is that the only way for many of them to care for their children, or themselves, with their husbands away at war was to have a liaison with a German soldier.

This ill treatment would not be the fate of Coco Chanel. The natural assumption might be that someone who was so much in the public eye would be subjected to the same, if not much worse, treatment as any other woman who had openly cavorted with a member of the Third Reich. In reality, the worst that Coco Chanel got was a few days of minor inconvenience.

It was August of 1944 and the allied troops were approaching Paris; the region was about to be completely freed from Nazi control. Chanel didn't remain in Paris during the allied liberation. According to her former maid, Germaine, Chanel got a call from someone passing on a secret message from the Duke of Westminster. The Duke was warning Chanel to get out of France urgently. In a matter of hours Coco was fleeing to Lausanne, Switzerland. There has been talk that Winston Churchill was responsible for shielding Chanel from much of the post-war fervour, while other sources suggest that her connections within the royal family may have had an impact in protecting certain members of the Windsor family's Nazi collaborations.

Chanel didn't face a judge or jury until 1946, when Judge Serre and his team put together documents that tied Chanel and her codename of

'Westminster' to the Nazis. They were unable to find any documented proof of information, or tangible advantages that Chanel had actually achieved for the Nazi party, so they were unable to issue an immediate warrant for her arrest. They did, however, issue a bench warrant for her to appear and explain herself and her extensive involvement and connections with the Germans. Judge Roger Serre issued a warrant on 16 April 1946, demanding that the police and the French border patrols bring her in to answer for the claims made by Baron Vaufreland when he was being interrogated. Chanel wouldn't appear in court for years, and not in front of Judge Serre.

Chanel finally answered the call a few years later to explain her actions during the war and about her connection to known Nazi conspirator and French traitor Baron Louis de Vaufreland. It turns out that in some of her travels she was paired with the Baron. Vaufreland bore the tag 'V-Mann' in his Abwehr files, which indicated that he had the trust of the Gestapo. The job that Vaufreland undertook was primarily recruitment of men and women who could be convinced or coerced into becoming spies for the Nazis. Apparently, Chanel would travel along with Vaufreland, in order to help conceal his actions. Vaufreland faced trial on 12 July 1949 for crimes against the French people by aiding the enemy during wartime. Coco Chanel was brought to testify during the trial and while she admitted to knowing Vaufreland, she downplayed their association and denied any wrong-doing. The prosecuting attorney, fixated on Vaufreland rather than Chanel, didn't press her very hard during her testimony. She then returned to her safe haven in Switzerland, while Vaufreland was found guilty and sentenced to six years in prison.

Biographer Hal Vaughn speculated in his book, *Sleeping with the Enemy: Coco Chanel's Secret War,* that Chanel might have paid off a former Nazi after the war. According to Vaughn, when former Nazi SS head of foreign intelligence, Walter Schellenberg, was looking to release his memoirs, and in an effort to suppress the book, Chanel paid him and his family off. Schellenberg, of course, had intimate knowledge of Chanel's involvement with the Nazis.

Later In Life

Coco Chanel had the luxury of living out the rest of her life in freedom, having never been truly taken to task for her actions during the war. She remained successful and outspoken, giving several interviews over the years that would contradict each other about various events in her life.

On 10 January 1971, Chanel died in the Hotel Ritz, the lavish home she enjoyed during the Nazi occupation of Paris. She was 87 years old.

The Chanel Brand Today

When Hal Vaughn's salacious book, *Sleeping with the Enemy: Coco Chanel's Secret War*, outright accused Coco of being a Nazi spy, the Chanel fashion house decided to reply in a press release. A representative for the fashion house said the following:

> *What's certain is that she had a relationship with a German aristocrat during the War. Clearly it wasn't the best period to have a love story with a German even if Baron von Dincklage was English by his mother and she (Chanel) knew him before the War.*

On the subject of Coco Chanel being perceived as an anti-Semite, the House of Chanel has said the following:

> *She would hardly have formed a relationship with the family of the owners or counted Jewish people among her close friends and professional partners such as the Rothschild family, the photographer Irving Penn or the well-known French writer Joseph Kessel had these really been her views.*

Chapter Six

Bayer: Heroin and Genocide

The history of Bayer is one that can only be described as complex and troubled. We've all heard of heroin, one of the most dangerous and addictive drugs in the world. The very mention of heroin can inspire images of underweight junkies, needles, and arms covered in track marks. The reality of heroin is that it causes an immense amount of suffering for the users and their loved ones. What you may not think about when you picture heroin is a bottle of the drug on a store shelf. Imagine heroin bottled by Bayer, the makers of aspirin, and marketed as a cough remedy for children. This was the reality a little over a century ago. Then, imagine for a moment that the creation and introduction of heroin was only a drop in the bucket, as the same company would be a co-sponsor of the Nazi concentration camps during the Second World War.

An Early History of Opioids

The origins of opium date as far back as 3400 BCE in the ancient region of Mesopotamia. The opium poppy was also found referenced in ancient texts from Egyptian, Sanskrit, Greek, Minoan and Sumerian cultures. The Sumerians would refer to it as the aptly named 'hul gil', which means 'plant of joy'. During the nineteenth century, when the Wild West of America was being settled and the railroad was under construction, a lot of immigrant workers were imported from China. These Chinese labourers brought with them opium, a substance that would catch on like wildfire. The images we see projected on film of a cowboy at the saloon drinking whiskey may have been a common sight in the movies and on television, but it was perhaps even more common in real life to find legendary characters like Wild Bill Hickock in a dimly lit opium den, high out of his mind.

The next stage in the story of opium was morphine. Originally named morphium, for the Greek god Morpheus (the god of dreams), the alkaloid that would become morphine was first isolated from the opium poppy by pharmacist's apprentice Friedrich Sertürner sometime between 1803 and 1805. It was the very first time any alkaloid had been isolated from a plant.

Morphine was later introduced to the marketplace for consumption by Merck in 1827. It was the shortcomings in morphine that would lead to the creation of heroin.

Medicine vs Snake Oils

You've no doubt heard the term 'snake oil' or 'snake oil salesman', at least in passing. While it's a cliché for a hoax nowadays, these elixirs were a very real and commonly used cure-all remedy throughout the 1700s and 1800s. The Victorian era was rife with quack medicine that made all sorts of claims, none of which needed to be proved by any government regulation until 1858 in the United Kingdom, and after the turn of the twentieth century in the United States.

When we think about snake oil today, what often comes to mind is a placebo or a hoax medicine that doesn't actually work. That wasn't necessarily always the case. While we didn't have a lot of the established medicines in the nineteenth century that we have now, many of the remedies that were used did have a medical basis. Bayer would initially market their heroin product like snake oil, which will be explored later in this chapter.

A few of the more famous, or rather infamous, snake oils were 'Richard Stoughton's elixir', 'Worner's Famous Rattlesnake Oil' and 'Clark Stanley's Snake Oil'. Richard Stoughton's elixir was one of the first bitters to receive a patent in England, back in 1712. The ingredients are said to have included the rinds of oranges, an ounce of gentian scraped and sliced, a sixpenny worth of cochineal and a pint of brandy. Gentian was often used for flavouring various bitters and is said to assist with digestive issues. The cochineal was most likely used to dye the mixture. Worner's Famous Rattlesnake Oil was said to cure rheumatism, paralysis, stiff joints, contracted cords and muscles, lumbago, pneumonia, neuralgia, deafness, asthma and catarrh. The claims made by Worner were clearly absurd and unfounded.

Clark Stanley's Snake Oil Liniment boasted quite a few more remedies, including general pain and lameness, rheumatism, neuralgia, sciatica, lame back, lumbago, contracted cords, toothache, strains, swellings, frost bites, chilblains, bruises, sore throat and even bites from animals, insects and reptiles! When the mixture was finally tested by the United States government in 1917, it was found to simply contain ingredients similar to a liniment or chest rub.

There became a need to regulate a great number of industries by the late nineteenth century, and one of those was the medicine trade. A good number of remedies may have had some slight means of medicinal assistance to them, but the reality is that a greater number were a complete sham and were sometimes more harmful than good. The regulation of drugs was so very dire not just because of the unregulated bitters, but due to the chemists offering what we still consider to be hard drugs today.

In Victorian Britain the attitude towards what we now consider to be illegal or subversive drugs was drastically different. The average chemist's shop would offer a number of drugs, including opium and cocaine. The Industrial Revolution was a time of great change, but also a time of increased drug use, not only by the working classes, but also the artists and writers of the era. An opium or morphine addiction wasn't as uncommon as it ought to have been.

It was near the latter half of the nineteenth century that a German chemist would create what he thought would be a cough remedy with pain relieving effects but without the addictive properties of morphine or codeine. It was through these noble intentions that one of the most terribly addictive drugs in the world today would be accidentally created.

The History of Bayer

The history of the company known as Bayer AG dates back to 1863, when the company was founded in Barmen, Germany. The first major mark that Bayer made on the world was when they copyrighted and sold aspirin, a product they are still known for today. The chemists at Bayer were hard at work developing their synthetically modified version of salicin, which they would eventually copyright as aspirin in 1897. Aspirin would enjoy a huge share of the marketplace, until two options with less side effects were introduced, acetaminophen in 1956 and ibuprofen in 1969.

There was controversy within Bayer early on, beginning with the true identity of the chemist who developed aspirin. The record books state that German Felix Hoffmann was responsible for the product, but those claims have been refuted by Arthur Eichengrun, a Jewish chemist who also worked for Bayer at the time. His claim is that once the company became entwined with the Nazi party during the Second World War, he was written out of the record books. The facts are that no documents prior to 1934 actually credit Hoffman with the invention. A company like Bayer, who had merged at the time with IG Farben, was very involved with the Nazi party in Germany, and therefore had every motivation to participate in an 'Aryanisation' of their history, especially when it comes to their most famous product. The idea that a Jewish chemist would be replaced in their records isn't outside the realm of possibility.

Who created Heroin?

The creation of heroin was truly without any intended malice, even though the end result would come to be a blight on society that would be felt well over a century later. A chemist named C. R. Alder Wright was the first person responsible for synthesising diacetylmorphine, now commonly known as heroin back in 1874. The British chemist came upon the mixture while he was experimenting with combining morphine with various acids. His results were recorded, but nothing more came of it at the time. This wasn't the point at which the world would be introduced to heroin.

The real introduction of the drug wouldn't happen until twenty-three years later at a Bayer pharmaceuticals factory in Wuppertal, North-Western Germany. A Bayer chemist by the name of Felix Hoffmann, the same one that was credited with aspirin, was the man responsible for the drug. He was instructed by his supervisor, Heinrich Dreser, to produce a more effective substitute for codeine for the pharmaceutical company. There were issues with the addictive properties in codeine, so Bayer was looking for an all-new non-addictive alternative to introduce into the marketplace.

The result of Hoffman's work would not, ironically, produce codeine, but rather a drug that is actually far less potent and more highly addictive than morphine, not to mention two and a half times more potent! The drug that would become known and marketed as heroin, was originally referred to as 'Heroisch', the German word for 'Heroic'. The name was a reference to the elevated emotional state that Bayer discovered the drug induced in its user. The emergence of the formula by Hoffman would lead to Bayer pioneering the commercialisation of heroin around the world. The drug was marketed as a non-addictive medicinal alternative to morphine and codeine; a claim that we are now well aware was false.

The testing phase began immediately and was conducted mostly with rabbits and frogs, but soon moved to human trials. The drug was tested on various Bayer employees and even on Hoffman himself. The next stage involved Dreser presenting heroin to the Congress of German Naturalists and Physicians in November of 1898. Dreser touted the drug as a miracle cure for coughs that was ten times more effective than codeine, with ten times fewer side effects, and none of the habit-forming properties. Bayer trademarked its original 'wonder drug' in 1898 and would soon market it to families worldwide.

Dr Bernard Lazarus did his own analysis of heroin, which he published in the *Boston Medical and Surgical Journal,* in 1900. In this he cited seven cases in which the use of heroin hydrochloride for the relief of coughs, especially in the case of tuberculosis, was an effective option. He goes on to state: 'The very thorough investigations which I have made with heroin hydrochloride in my practice enable me impartially to state that I consider this drug a most valuable aid to the medical profession.'

Why Heroin? The Purpose and Cures

In our age of modern medical achievements we may ask ourselves why would any parent turn to a dangerous drug like heroin as a cough remedy for their children? The reputation of heroin is well established today, but back in the late nineteenth century it was a brand-new product, without the horrific reputation it carries today. Bayer was simply filling the need that was left in the marketplace to address the mortal fear of the dreaded cough. When a child came down with a cough in this pre-vaccination era it was a frightening situation for their parents. There was an intense, but very well founded, fear of a deadly disease striking, such as tuberculosis, pneumonia or pertussis (aka whooping cough). The death toll from tuberculosis in the United States alone back in 1900 was nearly 150,000 per annum. The prevalent thought process at the time was that the intense cough was the symptom that would lead to the disease. We now know that is not the case, but the desire to prevent and eliminate a cough once it surfaced, and to eliminate coughing fits while one was trying to rest, was one that companies were happy to try and satisfy through various remedies and products.

Heroin Marketed to Children

It was all the way back on 6 March 1899 when Bayer first patented aspirin (acetylsalicylic acid) with the Imperial Patent Office in Berlin, but for decades now, the company has been promoting the medicine as a preventative for heart attacks and this has become a major selling point for aspirin products. It is common knowledge nowadays that taking a low-dose aspirin each day can prevent a heart attack or stroke. The blood-thinning medication can help to keep blood clots from forming.

Bayer has branded their aspirin with motivational, and telling, slogans such as 'The More You Know, The More You Trust Bayer', and 'Take it for Pain, Take it for Life'. Their most recent, as of the writing of his book, was 'Expect Wonders'. In fact, they continue to label their aspirin as a pro-heart 'wonder drug'. Bayer has marketed their aspirin this way, but the reality of a

Bayer aspirin regime is that it can reduce instances of a fatal heart attack by ten per cent and non-fatal heart attacks by twenty per cent, but it has been shown to increase gastrointestinal bleeding episodes in thirty per cent of users, according to a 2012 research study.

The marketing of their second major product, heroin-hydrochloride, persisted well into the twentieth century. A Bayer Pharmaceutical Products ad from 1901 markets the drug to pharmacies as a way to manufacture their own remedies like 'cough elixirs, cough balsams, cough drops, cough lozenges and cough medicines of any kind'. Bayer would also use the slogan: 'The Sedative For Coughs', to describe their heroin product. Vintage Bayer adverts in Spanish newspapers around 1912 featured ads that clearly market the use of heroin or 'heronia' to children. The adverts feature headlines such as 'la tos desaparece', which translates to 'cough disappears', and feature doting mothers administering the 'medicine' to their offspring.

The bottles were offered in 1oz quantities at a cost of $4.85 per ounce. Allowing for inflation, the cost would be just over $139 per ounce today. Bayer didn't limit their marketing of heroin as just a cough remedy however; they actually suggested it was a miracle cure-all that could be used for everything from schizophrenia to the common cold. Obviously, we know that none of these claims had any basis whatsoever, but snake oil marketing like this wasn't uncommon for the era and certainly wasn't limited to Bayer.

The thought of developing and marketing heroin to the public, much less children, seems particularly heinous. The question has to be asked, can we actually hold Bayer responsible? After all, we didn't know that heroin was such a dangerous and addictive drug back in those days, right? Unfortunately, that is not necessarily the case. Concerns were raised about the addictiveness of the drug very early on – as early as the year after its release. Bayer was well aware of this concern, but continued to market heroin to children well into the twentieth century. It wasn't until 1914 that the drug was finally restricted to a prescription-only medication by the Harrison Narcotics Tax Act. Heroin wouldn't be fully banned from sale and importation until 1924. If heroin were the darkest skeleton in Bayer's past it would be more than enough, but it is only the beginning of their twisted story.

Bayer and the Nazis

The creation and marketing of heroin to children could perhaps be enough to constitute a seriously dark past, but the skeletons in Bayer's closet seem to go far deeper than that.

During the Second World War there was a pharmaceutical conglomerate named IG Farben. The IG is short for the German word Interessengemeinschaft, which translates to 'Association of Common Interests'. IG Farben consisted of eight different companies, BASF, Hoechst, Agfa, Chemische Fabrik Griesheim-Elektron, Chemische Fabrik vorm. Weiler Ter Meer, Cassella, Chemische Fabrik Kalle and Bayer. Bayer wasn't just a part of the corporate machine, they were actually one of the major players in IG Farben with a 27.4 per cent equity capital investment. IG Farben employed hundreds of thousands of German citizens by the late 1930s and would become the single largest Germany exporter, enjoying a monopoly in the marketplace.

IG Farben decided to go into business with Adolf HItler and his Nazi Party early on and enjoyed a long relationship with the future dictator. In fact, IG Farben would donate significant amounts of money to the National Socialist Party to support their political election campaigns. Adolf Hitler was appointed the German chancellor on 30 January 1933, after a failed attempt at a presidential run in 1932. This new position of power served only to embolden the Nazi Party and they quickly set their sights on the upcoming German elections to be held on 5 March 1933. The Nazis were hoping to gain a majority vote in the Reichstag, so that they could pass the Enabling Act. The Act was a Weimar Constitutional amendment that would give Hitler the ability to enact laws on his own with the approval of the German Cabinet, effectively bypassing any approvals previously needed from the Reichstag. The Act, along with the preceding Reichstag Fire Decree, would pave the way for Hitler's dictatorship and absolute power in Germany.

A secret meeting was held on 20 February 1933 between Hitler and over two dozen powerful industrialists at Hermann Goering's home. The purpose behind the meeting was to persuade the big business moguls to invest in the Nazi Party election campaigns for the coming March. The donations came in from several companies, raising over two million Reichsmark, four hundred thousand of those Reichsmark coming from IG Farben alone. IG Farben was reportedly represented at the meeting by board member Georg von Schnitzler. Schnitzler later became a captain in the Nazi Sturmabteilung (aka the Brownshirts). In order to place that donation into context with inflation, that four hundred thousand Reichsmark would be the equivalent to around thirty million dollars (nearly twenty-four million pounds) today. The efforts were for nought, because the Nazis failed to obtain the majority they were seeking in that election. Instead, they rendered any Communist members of the Reichstag unable to vote and threatened any non-Nazi members with violence, winning the vote for the Enabling Act through intimidation.

It was only through the assistance of IG Farben that many of the medical and scientific horrors of the concentration camps were able to proceed. In 1940, IG Farben were looking to build a new factory and they set their sights on Himmler's largest concentration camp, built in Oswiecim, or Auschwitz, Poland. The site was scouted by Otto Ambros, who found it to be ideal. The plan was to utilise slave labour from the camp to construct their new plant. The result was the Farben Suschwitz plant. It was the financial involvement of IG Farben that took Auschwitz from an obscure backwater of the Nazi extermination plan and pushed it to the forefront, making it the site of one of the largest mass murders in history.

When touring the grim and sorrowful remains of the Auschwitz concentration camp, the museum guides will plainly tell you that IG Farben were behind the Nazis building the Birkenau camp. The camp began, not as an extermination camp like so many others, but as a slave labour camp for IG Farben Industries. Slave labour was an integral part of the Nazi regime, with many companies taking part in the dark practice. The Buna Industrial plant, known as IG Auschwitz, was located approximately 6km from the Auschwitz camp. Buna housed one hundred thousand Soviet prisoners of war and utilised them for slave labour.

The Polish farmers who had been living on the land where the Auchwitz complexes would be constructed were all kicked-off of the land, all of their property destroyed to make way for the death and labour camps in 1940 and 1941. The Nazis utilised some of the raw leftover materials after the farmers' buildings were destroyed as part of the construction of the camps. It wasn't until after the Wannsee Conference in 1942 that thousands of innocent Western European Jews were shipped to Birkenau to be slaughtered or enslaved. IG Farben built an industrial complex on the land near Auchwitz to produce their chemicals; thirty thousand slave labourers would die there. When the Adolf Hitler was gearing-up to invade Poland and Czechoslovakia, IG Farben was working closely with the Nazis to secure and seize desired chemical plants in those regions. The conditions within Auschwitz were deplorable. The clothing and living spaces would often become infected with lice or other vermin and when that happened, a deadly chemical fumigant known as Zyklon B was used to treat them and kill the infecting creatures. In fact, the Zyklon B chemical fumigant gas would end up being the method used to kill the Russians, Jews, Gypsies and other prisoners in the Nazi gas chambers. The Nazis were in search of a more economically efficient way to mass-murder their prisoners and it was Auschwitz deputy Karl Fritzsch who first thought up the idea of using the gas to kill humans in the camp. This gas was produced by Fritz Haber's company, Degesch (Deutsche Gesellschaft fur Schadlingsbekampfung). Degesch utilised the evil product under licence from IG Farben who, in turn, owned 42.2 per cent of the shares in Degesch. Experiements that IG Farben were involved in included the forced testing of drugs on prisoners – including what would become the first round of chemotherapy treatments. Nazi SS Major Dr med. Helmuth Vetter was an employee of IG Farben. Vetter was the notorious chief doctor at Auschwitz and was himself often responsible, along with the other doctors there, for selecting which Jews would face the gas chambers. The Nazi SS Dr Hoven would testify the following at the Nuremberg trials:

> *It should be generally known, and especially in German scientific circles, that the SS did not have notable scientists at its disposal. It is clear that the experiments in the concentration camps with IG preparations only took place in the interests of the IG, which strived by all means to determine the effectiveness of these preparations. They let the SS deal with the – shall I say – dirty work in the concentration camps. It was not the IG's intention to bring any of this out in the open, but rather to put up a smoke screen around the experiments so that (…) they could keep any profits to themselves. Not the SS but the IG took the initiative for the concentration camp experiments.*

Bayer After the Second World War

The Allies broke up the IG Farben conglomerate in 1945. Unlike so many of the companies that were involved with the Nazi regime during the Second World War, IG Farben didn't come away unaffected. Their direct involvement with the atrocities of war earned twenty-four members of the company a spot in the famed Nuremberg trials.

Although there were twenty-four intended defendants, one was excused from the trials due to a serious illness. The twenty-three members of IG Farben who actually stood trial for their war crimes inluded Carl Krauch (Chairman of the Supervisory Board), Hermann Schmitz (Chairman of the Managing Board), Georg von Schnitzler (Military Economy Leader), Fritz Gajewski (Director of AGFA), Heinrich Horein (Head of chemical research), August von Knieriem (Chief Counsel and Head of the legal department), Fritz ter Meer (Head of Department II), Christian Schneider (Head of

Department I), Otto Ambros (Buna plant production chief), Paul Hafliger (Head of the metals dept.), Ernst Burgin (Plant leader), Carl Lautenschlager (Plant leader), Max Ilgner (Head of intelligence and propaganda), Heinrich Butefisch (Production chief at Auschwitz), Friedrich Jahne (Chief engineer), Hans Kugler (Head of sales for dyestuffs), Heinrich Gattinau (Intelligence and plant police), Carl Wurster (Plant leader), Hans Kuhne (Plant leader), Wilhelm Rudolf Mann (Pharmaceuticals), Heinrich Oster (Manager of the Nitrogen Syndicate), Walter Durrfeld (Head of construction at Auschwitz and Monowitz) and Erich von der Heyde (Deputy of intelligence and plant police). A good number of the men on trial were also members of the Nazi SS and SA at various levels.

The trial began on 27 August 1947 and ran for nearly a year, until 11 June 1948. The IG Farben Trial was the third longest trial held at Nuremberg, behind the IMT trial and the Ministries Case. The judges who served as part of the Military Tribunal VI and oversaw the trial included Clarence F. Merril, Paul M. Herbert, James Morris and Curtis Grover Shake.

On the first day of the trial the prosecuting attorney's opening statement addressed the kind of charges that were being levied against the twenty-four men. The following is quoted directly from the transcript of that opening statement:

The grave charges in this case have not been laid before the Tribunal casually or unreflectingly. The indictment accuses these men of major responsibility for visiting upon mankind the most soaring and catastrophic war in modern history. It accuses them of wholesale enslavement, plunder and murder. These are terrible charges... The crimes with which these man are charged were not committed in rage, or under the stress of sudden temptation; they were not the slips or lapses of otherwise well-ordered men. One does not build a stupendous war machine in a fit of passion, nor an Auschwitz factory during a passing spasm of brutality. What these men did was done with the utmost deliberation and would, I venture to surmise, be repeated if the opportunity should recur. There will be no mistaking the ruthless purposefulness with which the defendants embarked upon their course of conduct.

The heaviest sentences were carried out for Otto Ambros and Walter Durrfeld, both of whom were directly related to the construction and running of the Auschwitz factory. They each received eight years' imprisonment. Fritz ter Meer would receive a seven-year sentence for his involvement in the chemical plant in Buna. Carl Krauch and Heinrich Butefisch both got six years and it went down from there. Ten of the men were actually acquitted of all charges and all of the men who were sentenced were given the luxury of time served as part of their sentencing.

The only apology from Bayer for their involvement with the Auschwitz death camps would come in 1995 to Nobel Prize winning author and holocaust survivor, Elie Wiesel. Elie had lost his mother and sister in the camps, but he himself was able to go on. He wrote a powerful first-hand account in his book titled simply *Night*, which has become required reading in many schools around the world. Elie had been scheduled in late 1995 to give a speech for the Three Rivers Lecture Series in Pittsburgh, Pennsylvania. He soon discovered that Bayer was one of the corporate sponsors of the event, and having full and intimate first-hand knowledge of what IG Farben had done to his family and so many others, he promptly cancelled the appearance. When the then president and CEO of Bayer, Helge H. Wehmeier, heard about the cancellation he personally paid a visit to Wiesel at his home. Wiesel recalled the visit to the *Pittsburgh Post-Gazette*, 'I was very moved by the man. I explained to him the situation. And I said to him: "Look, Bayer never apologized". I said it straight out. 'And he said, "What if I apologize?" Right then, I knew he would do it, and do it well'.

Apologise he did; Wehmeier included an apology as a foreword to Elie's speech, which included remarks about his 'shock and shame' at what his company had done in conjunction with the Nazis. He went on to express that he felt 'the obligation, but also the opportunity, to shape a different future, a better understanding and a better world'. Wiesel, for what it's worth, found no blame with Wehmeier himself and said so during his speech, 'It's not your fault that IG Farben was guilty.' Wehmeier himself wasn't even born until 1943. The apology was certainly a step in the right direction, but unfortunately time would tell that the feelings of regret were more Wehmeier's than those of Bayer AG.

It would be natural to assume that Bayer would want to continue to distance themselves from the IG Farben days as much as possible after the fallout from the Second World War, even after Helge Wehmeier retired in 2004. Unfortunately, just two years later, Bayer would be back to endorsing the dark side of their history. In 1956, Second World War criminal Fritz ter Meer had been appointed the chairman of the supervisory board of Bayer. Fritz had been the head officer directing the operations of IG Farben Auschwitz and was sentenced to seven years for his part in the horrors;

a sentence of which he would serve only four years. Fritz held the position at Bayer for seven years – three years longer than he spent in prison for his war crimes. Bayer AG seemed to reinforce this piece of their dark history in 2006 when, despite Wehmeier's earlier apology, they sponsored a large memorial wreath on the grave of ter Meer.

Bayer Today and Modern Controversy

Bayer has a history steeped in controversy and horror, and the company seems unable to stay away from the negative spotlight even today. The CBG Network or Coordination gegen Bayer-Gefahren (translation: Coalition against Bayer-Dangers) was established as a watchdog group that minds the activities of Bayer. The company has continued to be rife with controversy around the world.

In 2006, the CBG Network found that Bayer's claims of significant greenhouse-gas emission reductions were unfounded, blatantly false, and spun with disinformation. They also noted in 2011 that Bayer CropScience was finally ceasing production of their most deadly pesticides. Philipp Mimkes from the Coalition against BAYER Dangers comments:

> *This is an important success for environmental organisations from all over the world who have fought against these deadly pesticides for decades. But we must not forget that Bayer broke their original promise to withdraw all class I products by the year 2000. Many lives could have been saved. It is embarrassing that the company only stopped sales because the profit margins of these chemical time bombs have fallen so much.*

The release by the CBG Network also noted:

> *Bayer has a world market share in pesticides of 20%. The WHO estimates the number of people who are poisoned by pesticides at three to 25 million per year. At least 40,000 people are killed accidentally by pesticides and the estimated number of unreported cases is much higher. Bayer products contribute enormously to the millions of poisonings each year.*

Bayer has also experienced issues with their various medications being found as a danger, such as the once popular birth control medicine

Yaz/Yasmin. The pill was found to contain drospirenone, which significantly elevates the risk of embolism or thrombosis in those who take it. The Bayer Pharma AG product Xarelto has also come under fire. The CBG Network discussed the dangers of the drug in 2012: Concerns regarding the safety of the anticoagulant Xarelto have not been dispelled. Trials carried out with the drug have resulted in a number of fatalities. Dubious practices are also being used to market the product. There are justified fears that a high-risk, over-expensive product with no additional therapeutic benefit is being forced onto the market. The BAYER Board of Management bears responsibility for this.

Christiane Schnura from the Coalition against BAYER Dangers:

> *The numerous reports of vascular occlusion, bleeding, cardiovascular problems and liver damage make it inadvisable to use Xarelto on a wide scale for the prevention of stroke. Products that do not offer any advantage compared with older products should on principle not be given regulatory approval.*

Xarelto was recalled temporarily in 2014 due to an issue with contamination and many lawsuits are still in the court system over the dangers of the drug.

The continued denial of any dark past by Bayer was also highlighted by the CBG Network in 2013:

> *On August 1, 1863 businessman Friedrich Bayer and dyer Johann Friedrich Weskott founded the company 'Friedr. Bayer et comp'. They initially produced synthetic dyestuffs but the range of products grew significantly over the years. In 1881, BAYER was made a joint stock corporation and developed into an international chemical company. In 1925 the firm became part of the IG FARBEN conglomerate.*

For its 150th anniversary BAYER organised numerous celebrations. More than 1,000 guests attended an event in Cologne, including German Chancellor Angela Merkel and North Rhine-Westphalian State Premier Hannelore Kraft. A specially built airship is promoted the company on all five continents. However, the unpleasant periods of the company's history were totally omitted from the celebrations. Topics such as environmental contamination, pesticide poisoning, worker protests and collaboration with the Third Reich were simply ignored.

Philipp Mimkes from the Coalition against BAYER Dangers said:

Being a part of the infamous IG Farben, BAYER was involved in the cruellest crimes in human history. A subsidiary supplied Zyklon B for the gas chambers. The company built a giant new factory directly at Auschwitz. To accommodate the slave workers, the corporation operated its own concentration camp. More than 30,000 labourers were worked to death. The company's commitment to supply fuel, munitions and rubber was vital for Hitler to wage international war.

Chapter Seven

Kellogg's: Corn Flakes and the War On Sex

Nineteenth century ideas about living 'the good life' once involved an inordinate amount of consumption and excess, and with that inevitably came poor health. This trend meant that health concerns were a huge part of the developing world near the end of the nineteenth century. It is difficult to imagine the terror that must have come with most illness in the era before vaccines and modern medicine. There was a widespread distrust of doctors in that time, and who could blame them? The practice of medicine was often as, or even more, barbaric and painful than the diseases that could ail you. We often hear people talking about 'quack-medicine' nowadays in a novelty sense, but looking back, pretty much all medical practice in the past has the appearance of quack medicine.

It was from this era of decadence that a need was born for a healthier way of living. There were several visionaries in the forefront of this movement, but few as famous, or rather infamous, as Dr John Harvey Kellogg. John Harvey and his younger brother, Will Keith, put their collective minds together to create a healthy food substitute, a cereal flake that would someday become known as Corn Flakes. The role of this rather plain dietary flake was to help one live a pure and healthy existence, but the history that surrounds it is anything but bland. The man behind the most famous breakfast cereal in America was also ardently in support of abstinence from masturbation, sexual arousal and sexual intercourse of any kind. He was also a ecumenist and a racial purist. The breakfast cereal revolution was about to begin and the two Kellogg brothers would be divided forever by the opposing forces of fanaticism and greed over a distinctly American breakfast icon.

The Early Life of John Harvey Kellogg

A young John Harvey Kellogg was the fifth son of humble Michigan frontier parents, John Preston and Anne Kellogg. Times were hard, but the Kellogg family kept their faith in God while they struggled to find their way. John was born on 26 February 1852 in Tyrone Township, a small Michigan rural community. John was a rather sickly child, being stricken by tuberculosis, which was often a death sentence in those days. The prolific disease wouldn't have a vaccine until 1921 and wouldn't be utilised on a wide scale until the 1950s. The stifling disease would keep John Harvey out of school until he was 9 years of age.

There is a story that is often re-told about John witnessing a boyhood friend being bled on a table right in front of him. John Harvey was so disturbed by the sight of the boy's blood, he exclaimed to his mother that he when he grew up, he wanted to be anything but a doctor. The statement is almost ironic; John Harvey Kellogg was not a doctor in the same way as the 'professionals' who had fumbled through medicine before him. No, John Harvey would be a whole new type of doctor, practising what was, for that time, a revolutionary new way of thinking; one he would personally help pioneer and make famous.

The Kelloggs eventually moved to Battle Creek, Michigan, where his father, without much enthusiasm, began the task of manufacturing brooms, a venture that proved to be a more successful avenue for the family. The Kellogg boys would soon join their father at work in the broom factory. Not everyone in those days, just as it is now, was cut out for the physical labour and long hours of factory work. It was during this time as a teenager that John Harvey realised he was not cut out for a life of manual labour. John, who had spent much of his youth in a frail state, was far more of a reader and preferred delving into a good book to working with his hands. His aspirations inspired him to become a school teacher, a perfectly noble and viable profession of the era, but one he would never pursue.

Instead, John found himself on the path to addressing and treating matters of health and wellbeing. It was religion that brought this new path into Kellogg's life. The Kellogg family, as it turns out, had become devout followers of the Seventh Day Adventist church, a new religion that had branched off from the Millerism movement. The followers of Millerism were still struggling to reform and find their way after the very specific 'second coming of Jesus' event, which their leader had pivoted their beliefs on, never took place. The event, referred as the 'Great Disappointment' was supposed to have taken place on 22 October 1844.

The Kelloggs were so involved in the Adventist Church that they donated a portion of the proceeds from the sale of their home when they moved from Tyrone Township to Battle Creek to fund the Adventist Church when they moved their publishing activities from Rochester, New York, to Battle Creek. The Kellogg family may have been in financial support of the Church, but John Harvey took his involvement to a far deeper level.

The Adventist Church had only a handful of leaders who helped with its formation; two of the more prominent were James and Ellen G. White.

The Whites were a major influencing force within the Adventist movement and the prophetic visions that Ellen White claimed to experience were frequent and taken as gospel, not only into how they should be living their lives and forming the religion, but sometimes even foretelling the future. Ellen's visions moved those who followed the religion towards keeping their body pure by rejecting many drinks, such as alcohol, coffee, and even tea. The entire Adventist movement also became vegetarian, feeling that eating the flesh of animals was an unclean act that would further serve to harm their bodies. The main theme of the religion was to truly purify the body. The original hope was that if the followers made their bodies and minds as pure as possible, then it might invite the second coming of Jesus Christ. The Adventists explained away the Great Disappointment by deciding that they were too unclean to be in the presence of the Lord, so their great quest of purity was everything to them.

John Harvey Kellogg was the source of one of Ellen's 'visions'. Ellen White came to her husband and explained that she had experienced a vision from God, which revealed to her that John Harvey Kellogg would someday be a very important part of their movement. It was from this moment forward that the Whites and the Adventist movement began to invest heavily in John Harvey's future, something that would change his life, and the world, forever.

In 1864 the 12-year-old John Harvey Kellogg officially began working for the Adventist church, printing and distributing propaganda pamphlets. James White took John Harvey under his wing and taught him the ins and outs of the church's publishing venture. One of the primary subjects of the Adventist pamphlets was Ellen White's articles on health and wellbeing. It was during this time that Kellogg would gain interest in the subject of the human body, since it was his job to set the type for the articles.

At the age of 14 John Harvey devoted himself to becoming a vegetarian, a vow that he would sustain for the rest of his life. That same year, on 5 September 1866, the Adventists opened a convalescent home, called the Western Health Reform Institute in Battle Creek. He didn't know it at the time, but this moment would become integral in Kellogg's life, because it was there that he would make his lasting mark on the world and start a whole new industry that still goes strong today.

Medical Training

In an effort to affirm and validate their beliefs, the Seventh Day leadership opted to begin sending select devoted young men within their movement to various schools for professional training in the medical field. The Whites personally chose John Harvey Kellogg to attend a five-month course at Dr Russell Trall's Hygeio-Theraputic College in 1872. Russell Trall was a trained allopath (a doctor with traditional training) who advocated alternative medical practices over traditional medication. Instead of regarding the human body as a physiological system, he firmly believed that it was an entity belonging to, and governed by, God. He subscribed to the school of thought that illness would occur when the natural laws of God were broken, basically that the sickness of the body was directly connected to sickness of the spirit. Dr Trall's Hygeio-Theraputic College wasn't so much a medical school, but rather an institute where he started to teach the ways of homeopathy and the benefits of diet and lifestyle in health over medicine or legitimate medical practice. His college was very forward thinking for the time, as the first of its kind in America to allow women an equal chance to learn alongside men. In fact, his enrolment comprised of nearly one third women.

Kellogg attended the course for five months, but he came away unimpressed with the alternative practices such as hydrotherapy that were being used. The practices he was taught also included having the patient consume forty to fifty glasses of water per day, and cleansing their bodies with water both inside and out.

In the modern world it can take upwards of eight years to earn a medical degree in the United States, but in John Harvey's day it wasn't such a meticulous process. It took him only two years to earn his MD from Bellevue Hospital Medical School in New York in 1875. The Whites served yet again as John Harvey's benefactors, loaning him the money to attend medical school. Dr Kellogg went on to spend time in London and Vienna after he obtained his medical degree, where he earned his surgical certification, learning the most updated techniques of the era. Surgery would remain a large part of the doctor's career, as he would perform over 22,000 operations.

The Battle Creek Sanitarium

The Adventists Western Health Reform Institute wasn't going as planned; with business failing, the Whites called upon their star protégé for help. Their decision to make John Harvey superintendent of the home in 1876 was a moment that changed history.

Dr Kellogg returned home to Battle Creek and brought a new level of confidence and self-assurance along with him. In his first acts as superintendent he wasted no time in expanding the facilities and changing the name to the Battle Creek Sanitarium. The new staff he brought in all had proper medical training; Dr Kellogg expected nothing but excellence from his staff. It was then that he began moulding the Battle Creek Sanitarium after his own ideas about wellness, opting to offer fewer and fewer services like hydrotherapy, and introduce more 'modern' techniques, which were a mixture of his heightened healthy-living programme and actual medical science.

Dr Kellogg wasn't satisfied to simply run the Sanitarium, he sought complete control. He even began to manipulate and exploit Ellen White's visions by implanting his own scheme, which Kellogg referred to as his 'Battle Creek Idea'. It is said that he would implant his ideas in her mind while she was in a vulnerable trance state. Ellen would then repeat Kellogg's ideas as though they were her own. This manipulation was one way that John Harvey moved things in the direction of his own vision. He also came to serve as editor for the *Adventist Health Reformer* newsletter, which had a focus on pushing the Adventist health propaganda. Kellogg would change the name of the newsletter to *Good Health* in 1879. Throughout his career and tenure at Battle Creek, Dr Kellogg also wrote and published more than fifty books. He was determined to get his ideas out to the world through any and all means necessary.

It was under John Harvey's rule that the Sanitarium became a beacon of health and well-being and the largest of its kind in the world. 'The San', as it was commonly known, offered cures for all things that ailed you. It served as a cross between a getaway spa and a medical clinic. Guests were immediately x-rayed, probed, and thoroughly examined upon arrival, and then assigned a regimen of baths, massages, exercise and diet.

Life at Battle Creek

The American diet and lifestyle in the late nineteenth century was often excessively full of fat, causing many health concerns including stomach upsets, nervousness and indigestion (neurostenia and dyspepsia). The San had a vast regime of treatments for anything and everything that may have ailed you.

The treatments were vast and ever-developing, most of which would be considered rather odd, or even absurd, by today's standards. One of them included covering the underweight guests with sandbags; another option was rooms that featured tubes and systems to bring in fresh air and expel germs, and a cage that would relax the patient with static electricity. They were all the latest and most innovative treatments of the era.

Dr Kellogg did have a tendency to fixate rather passionately on a number of twisted pursuits however. One of the main focuses he had was his self-declared war on the human colon. He was obsessed to the extent that he actually wrote a 362-page book in 1915 titled *Colon Hygiene*, in which he explores the functions and possible treatments of the colon, up to and including removal. Kellogg felt passionately about the impurity and spiritual uncleanliness of the organ:

> *in the treatment of every chronic disease, and most acute maladies, the colon must be reckoned with. That the average colon, in civilized communities, is in a desperately depraved and dangerous condition, can no longer be doubted. The colon must either be removed or reformed.*

Kellogg treated thousands of patients at The San over the years, most of them with surgery, referring to it as, 'a hold of unclean and hateful parasites, a veritable Pandora's box of disease and degeneracy'. He firmly believed in the unclean nature of the colon:

> *That most despised and neglected portion of the body, the colon, has in recent years been made the subject of much scientific study and research, with the result that a lively controversy has been stirred up over the question as to whether this organ should be permitted to remain a part of the 'human form divine,' or whether it should be cast out as worse than useless and unworthy of place in the anatomy…*

Kellogg also firmly believed in the healing power of sunlight. A light machine that Kellogg invented was even showcased at the 1893 Chicago World's Fair. The machine utilised light bulbs to create heat and light intended to cure various diseases. He also believed that the colour white absorbed the sun, so he consistently wore all white clothing to help him absorb the full benefits that sunlight could offer. He would often utilise an Arc lamp to the scalp or ear as another way to absorb healing light.

Dr Kellogg invented a number of quack medical contraptions, which he was convinced would help his patients at The San. These included the electrotherapy exercise bed, medical slapping-massage machine, two and four person food vibrators, mechanical horses, the infamous Oscillomanipulator and the hot air bath. In fact, The San had an entire Vibro-Mechanical department. Kellogg also found that music inspired people to exercise and eliminated some of the boredom associated with the often tedious process. He even created early workout music recordings on phonograph to help inspire his patients.

Seen as a 'posh' medical retreat, The San enjoyed a number of famous patients, including playwright George Bernard Shaw, industrialist Henry Ford, wealthy businessman John D. Rockefeller, owner of the *Wall Street Journal* C.W. Baron and even a visit in 1927 from famed Olympic swimmer Johnny Weissmuller. Kellogg made good use of Weissmuller's visit and used him to create shadow-grams that would display his vision of the ideal human physique. Dr Kellogg got Weissmuller to follow a vegetarian diet while he was there and he actually broke one of his own records in the pools at The San pool, lending further legitimacy to Kellogg's programme.

John Harvey brought his younger brother, William Keith Kellogg, into the Battle Creek Sanitarium to help keep the books and run much of the business end, so he could fully focus on his health ideas and ambitions for The San. William had just recently completed a four-month business course and was the perfect candidate to help John Harvey, because he never really challenged his absolute authority. If you were to work at The San, then you could expect a salary of up to $9 per week. The first-year nurses were treated to room and board, but no salary. This wasn't an uncommon practice in the nineteenth century. Dr Kellogg felt the honour of working under him was enough compensation. John Harvey boasted that he himself took no salary, assumingly a testament to his dedication to the healthy cause, but the reality is that his speeches and books alone made him wealthy. Employees were also required to forego meat. This isn't a surprising requirement from the author of *Shall We Slay To Eat?* Kellogg believed that meat was the cause of many illnesses.

Kellogg was so serious about the health benefits of committing to a life of vegetarianism that he not only required it of his staff, but also of all guests of The San. Often, the patients were unable to commit fully to the programme and snuck away to indulge themselves and eat meat at a nearby restaurant. Dr Kellogg was apparently aware that this would occur and it frustrated him endlessly. The menus at The San included carefully chosen selections such as creamed cauliflower, celery, radishes, yogurt, cheese, stewed raisins, apple pie, bananas, good health biscuits, pineapple sauce and kaffir tea. No salt and sugar were offered as they were considered to be unnecessary and impure.

The daily menu would be printed at the Sanitarium and would include the programme for that day. Here is an example of one such programme, this specific one from 16 November 1927:

7.00 AM Gymnasium – Chest Gymnasics
7.20 AM Parlor – Morning Worship
7.40 to 8.40 AM Breakfast

8.30 to 9.00 AM Gymnasium – Special Class for Women, Folk Dances, etc.
9.00 to 9.30 AM Gymnasium – Drill and March for Men and Women
9.30 to 10.00 AM Gymnasium – Games, Baseball, etc., for men
12.45 to 2.00 PM Dinner
2.00 to 3.00 PM Lobby – Orchestra Concert
3.00 to 4.00 PM Gymnasium – Games, Medical Gymnastics, Volley Ball, etc.
6.00 to 6.45 PM Supper
7.00 PM Gymnasium – Light Gymnastics and Grand March with Music
8.00 PM Parlour – Lecture, Dr W. H. Riley

Kellogg continued to explore his distrust of the human colon by attempting to prove that constipation was a problem that only humans experienced and that it was somehow tied to their consumption of meat. He travelled widely to study animals and found that vegetarian animals would experience frequent bowel movements, so he decided that he would help his human patients to experience the same. Dr Kellogg created the Colonic Irrigation Machine to deal with this problem, which would wash out the digestive tract of the patient with warm water. It was Kellogg's commitment to changing the diets of his patients that would soon lead to him working to develop his own food alternatives.

Kellogg had all kinds of ideas about not just diet, but also human sexuality, marriage, and life. In 1879, he married Ella Ervilla Eaton; it is said that he enjoyed her intelligence, which is what attracted him to her. He boasted that he and his wife never consummated their marriage, in fact he spent their honeymoon writing a book. Kellogg and his wife would never have biological children of their own; instead they adopted over forty children from all around the world.

There were certainly medical theories in Dr Kellogg's writing that were profound and ahead of their time, but we are also forced to acknowledge a high level of the absurd in many of the assertions he put forth. Kellogg was convinced, for example, that marriage had a physical affect on a woman. If a woman had children with her second husband, Kellogg asserted that they would more closely resemble the first husband, rather than their biological father. He also believed that if a black woman had a baby with a white man, that all of her subsequent babies would be lighter in skin tone, even if their biological father was a black male. Kellogg also had strong feelings about who should and should not be able to marry; he believed, for example, that a criminal should never marry, neither should someone who is disproportionate in size, has a gap in age between the husband and wife and, to top it all off, he was also against interracial marriage.

The evils of sex also extended to the world of dance. Dr Kellogg was certain that 'round dances', like the Waltz, would lead to rampant immorality, such as late hours, fashionable dressing, midnight feats and improper dress. These violations of morality were something that he was utterly convinced would cause injury to the body, mind, and spirit.

It was Kellogg's views on sexuality, abstinence, and the evils of masturbation that would linger as his most ardent and resounding notions. The recurring theme in all of Kellogg's beliefs is purity and uncleanliness, both physical and mental. He would refer to the very notion of mental sexual arousal and the indulgence of those 'impure thoughts', as leading down the path of an 'immoral life' full of 'vicious habits'. Kellogg was so adamant about the evils of masturbation that one of his 'treatments' at The San included applying carbolic acid to the clitoris of female patients, and electro-shock to prevent the harmful practice of masturbation.

The evils of masturbation, or the 'solitary vice', were written about extensively by Dr Kellogg in his book *Plain Facts For Old And Young*:

> *If illicit commerce of the sexes is a heinous sin, self-pollution, or masturbation, is a crime doubly abominable. As a sin against nature, it has no parallel except in sodomy (see Gen. 19:5; Judges 19:22). It is the most dangerous of all sexual abuses because the most extensively practised. The vice consists in an excitement of the genital organs produced otherwise than in the natural way. It is known by the terms, self-pollution, self-abuse, masturbation, onanism, manustupration, voluntary pollution, and solitary or secret vice. The vice is the more extensive because there are almost no bounds to its indulgence. Its frequent repetition fastens it upon the victim with a fascination almost irresistible! It may be begun in earliest infancy, and may continue through life.*

A lot of the good doctor's passions regarding the evils of masturbation quickly gave way to embellishments and obvious fear tactics. A great example of this is seen when he goes on in his book to discuss a specific case of a young boy who was inflicted with the unclean habit:

> *Unsuspected Rottenness. — Parents who have no suspicion of the evil, who think their children the embodiment of purity, will find by careful observation and inquiry, — though personal testimony cannot be relied upon, -- that in many instances their supposed virtuous children are*

old in corruption. Such a revelation has brought dismay into many a family, in some cases only too late.

Not long since a case came under our care which well illustrates the apathy and blindness of parents with respect to this subject. The parents of a young man whose mind seemed to be somewhat disordered, sent word to us through a friend respecting his condition, asking advice. We suspected from the symptoms described the real cause of the disease, and urged prompt attention to the case. In a short time the young man was placed under our immediate care without encouragement of a cure, and we gave the case still closer study. The characteristic symptoms of disease from self-abuse were marked, but the father was positive that no influence of that kind could have been at work. He had watched his son narrowly from infancy, and did not believe it possible for him to have been guilty. In addition, the young man had long been remarkable for his piety, and he did not believe there could be any possibility of his being guilty of so gross a crime.

A short time sufficed, however, to secure the indisputable evidence of the fact by his being caught in the act by his nurse.

This young man was a sad example of what havoc is made with the 'human form divine' by this debasing vice. Once a bright boy, kind, affectionate, active, intelligent, the pride of a loving mother and the hope of a doting father, his mind had sunken to drivelling idiocy. His vacant stare and expressionless countenance betokened almost complete imbecility. If allowed to do so, he would remain for hours in whatever position his last movement left him. If his hand was raised, it remained extended until placed in a position of rest by his attendant. Only with the utmost difficulty could he be made to rise in the morning, to eat, drink, or walk. Only by great efforts could he be aroused from his lethargy sufficiently to answer the most simple question. The instinctive demands of decency in regarding the calls of nature were not respected. In short, the distinguishing characteristics of a human being were almost wholly obliterated, leaving but a physical semblance of humanity, -- a mind completely wrecked, a body undergoing dissolution while yet alive, a blasted life, no hope for this world, no prospect for the next. In the insane asylums of the country may be seen hundreds of these poor victims in all stages of physical and mental demoralisation.

Kellogg continues, using a lot of extreme terms for the causes of masturbation, such as 'wicked', 'evil', 'danger', 'corruption' and 'devastating'. He was convinced that the disease of self-abuse could lead to anything ranging from bladder stones and epilepsy to children emerging with sexual excitement from spanking or whipping.

This is all so very disconcerting, but fear not... it is easy for parents to control this danger in their children, according to Dr Kellogg. There are a grand total of thirty-nine suspicious warning signs to watch out for. In a final testament to the extent of Kellogg's pre-occupation with sex, please enjoy the following list. A warning to you the reader, these range from the contrary to the absurd and are taken directly from Dr Kellogg's own writing:

General debility, coming upon a previously healthy child, marked by emaciation, weakness, an unnatural paleness, colorless lips and gums, and the general symptoms of exhaustion, when it cannot be traced to any other legitimate cause, as internal disease, worms, grief, overwork, poor air, or poor food, and when it is not speedily removed by change of air or appropriate remedial measures, may be safely attributed to solitary vice, no matter how far above natural suspicion the individual may be. Mistakes will be rare indeed when such a judgment is pronounced under the circumstances named. Premature and defective development is a symptom closely allied to the two preceding. When it cannot be traced to such natural causes as overstudy, overwork, lack of exercise, and other influences of a similar nature, it should be charged to self-abuse. The early exercise of the genital organs hastens the attainment of puberty in many cases, especially when the habit is acquired early; but at the same time it saps the vital energies so that the system is unable to manifest that increased energy in growth and development which usually occurs at this period. In consequence, the body remains small, or does not attain that development which it otherwise would. The mind is dwarfed as well as the body. Sometimes the mind suffers more than the body in lack of development, and sometimes the reverse is true. This defective development is shown in the physical organization of males, in the failure of the voice to increase in volume and depth of tone as it should, in deficient growth of the beard, and in failure of the chest to become full and the shoulders broad. The mind and character show the dwarfing influence by failure to develop those qualities which especially distinguish a noble manhood. In the female, defective development is shown by menstrual derangements, by defective growth either in stature, or as shown in unnatural slimness, and in a failure to develop the graces and pleasing character which should distinguish early womanhood.

Such signs deserve careful investigation; for they can only result from some powerfully blighting influence.

Sudden change in disposition is a sign which may well arouse suspicion. If a boy who has previously been cheerful, pleasant, dutiful, and gentle, suddenly becomes morose, cross, peevish, irritable, and disobedient, be sure that some foul influence is at work with him. When a girl, naturally joyous, happy, confiding, and amiable, becomes unaccountably gloomy, sad, fretful, dissatisfied, and unconfiding, be certain that a blight of no insignificant character is resting upon her. Make a careful study of the habits of such children; and if there is no sudden illness to account for the change in their character, it need not require long deliberation to arrive at the true cause; for it will rarely be found to be anything other than solitary indulgence.

Failure of mental capacity without apparent cause, should occasion suspicion of evil practices. When a child who has previously learned readily, mastered his lessons easily, and possessed a retentive memory, shows a manifest decline in these directions, fails to get his lessons, becomes stupid, forgetful, and inattentive, he has probably become the victim of a terrible vice, and is on the road to speedy mental as well as physical ruin. Watch him. Untrustworthiness appearing in a child should attract attention to his habits. If he has suddenly become heedless, listless, and forgetful, so that he cannot be depended upon, though previously not so, lay the blame upon solitary indulgence. This vice has a wonderful influence in developing untruthfulness. A child previously honest, will soon become an inveterate liar under its baneful influence.

Mock piety -- or perhaps we should more properly designate it as mistaken piety -- is another peculiar manifestation of the effects of this vicious practice. The victim is observed to become transformed, by degrees, from a romping, laughing child, full of hilarity and frolic, to a sober and very sedate little Christian, the friends think, and they are highly gratified with the piety of the child. Little do they suspect the real cause of the solemn face; not the slightest suspicion have they of the foul orgies practised by the little sinner. By the aid of friends, he may soon add hypocrisy to his other crimes, and find in assumed devotion a ready pretence for seeking solitude. Parents will do well to investigate the origin of this kind of religion in their children.

Boys in whom the habit has become well developed, sometimes manifest a decided aversion to the society of girls; but this is not nearly so often the case as some authors seem to indicate. It would rather appear that the opposite is more often true. Girls usually show an increasing fondness for the society of boys, and are very prone to exhibit marked evidences of real wantonness.

Lack of development of the breasts in females, after puberty, is a common result of self-pollution. Still it would be entirely unsafe to say that every female with small mammary glands had been addicted to this vice, especially at the present time, when a fair natural development is often destroyed by the constant pressure and heat of "pads." But this sign may well be given a due bearing.

Biting the fingernails is a practice very common in girls addicted to this vice. In such persons there will also be found, not infrequently, slight soreness or ulceration at the roots of the nails, and warts, one or more, upon one or both the first two fingers of the hand, usually the right.

The eyes often betray much. If, in addition to want of lustre and natural brilliancy, they are sunken, present red edges, are somewhat sore, perhaps, and are surrounded by a dark ring, the patient, especially if a child, should be suspected and carefully watched. It should be observed, however, that dyspepsia, debility from any cause, and especially loss of sleep, will produce some or all of these signs, and no one should be accused of the vice upon the evidence of these indications alone; neither could he be justly suspected so long as his symptoms could be accounted for by legitimate causes.

These are, of course, only a few of the thirty-nine examples that Dr Kellogg provides. Upon reading the entire list it becomes clear that almost everything is a sign of self-abuse to Kellogg. It encompasses everything from round shoulders and paleness to acne and tobacco use. The list even contradicts itself at times by listing both boldness and bashfulness as potential signs. We know, of course, that symptoms like acne are brought on by puberty and hormones. It's hard to imagine how one man's preoccupation with self-abuse could change the world, but this path would leave Dr Kellogg in search of a remedy to help those that he felt were in dire need of assistance.

The creation of the Corn Flake

In 1877 Kellogg created the Sanitarium Health Food Company to develop and sell his vegetarian products. He and his brother William spent countless hours creating various foods and trying out ideas, such as Protose, a meat substitute that consisted mostly of peanuts and wheat gluten. One included NutButter, an early form of peanut butter, in which he would boil the nuts instead of roasting them. Kellogg was granted a patent specifically for the 'Process of Producing Alimentary Products' in 1898.

The need to deal with the unclean acts of sexuality and masturbation was a great weight on the mind of Dr Kellogg, so he and his younger brother went to work to create a special food that would satisfy the hunger of their patients, while dulling their sexual appetites. One food that the Kellogg brothers tried on the patients of The San was a form of shredded wheat. The concept of shredded wheat cereal was actually invented in 1890 down in Denver, Colorado, by a man named Henry Perky. Perky sold his dry, pillow-like biscuits to vegetarian restaurants and eventually expanded into distribution and production on the east coast of the United States by 1892. Kellogg was a purchaser of shredded wheat as an option for his patrons at The San, but the reception from the patients was unfavourable, judging it far too bland, so he never purchased the patent from Perky. William Keith would later purchase the patent when he split from his brother to create the Battle Creek Toasted Corn Flake Company.

The Kellogg brothers were determined to develop a flake cereal that offered significantly more taste, but was conducive to John Harvey's biologic living philosophy. It was hard for the brothers to get their flake-style cereal to take shape. In 1894, Corn Flakes were finally created and it was very much by accident. William had left for a few days to deal with his creative frustrations and think; when he returned, the batter they were using was mouldy, so he gave the crank a turn and out came the flakes. It turned out that the mould had given the batter the rise that it needed to form properly. The first flakes were made from wheat, but the concept would also work on rice, oats, and corn. William Keith stumbled upon the process, but John Harvey would claim the idea, insisting that it had come to him in a dream. The toasted flakes were to be sold exclusively to The San patients, and subscribers to their wellness magazine. The Kellogg brothers filed for a patent on 31 May 1895. The patent for 'Flaked Cereals and Process of Preparing Same' was granted on 14 April 1896.

It was quite clear early on that William Keith had aspirations to market their Corn Flakes product on a wider scale, but John Harvey was adamantly against the idea and forbade it. This was a divide that would change the relationship of the Kellogg brothers. The business sense of William Keith was in direct contradiction with the passion and dedication that John Harvey had to his beliefs.

Fate is a funny thing, to be sure. It turns out that Charles W. Post, the man who started the still prolific Post Cereal Company, was a regular at the Sanitarium. Starting in 1891 Post lived for extended periods at The San off and on for many years. It was while he was there that he saw the immense potential in the products being offered to patients. Prior to his ventures into cereal, Post was largely unsuccessful as a businessman. He created his own product called Postum, a coffee substitute, after observing the experiments and creations at The San. Kellogg didn't mind Post coming there and poaching their ideas, because he was far too concerned with his mission. Post would soon market Grape Nuts, which became a commercial success; he had made his first million by 1901 and his wild success became an annoyance to Dr Kellogg. Post had exceeded any expectations that Kellogg had had of him, and John Harvey would call Post an imitator of his ideas.

I could have accumulated a fortune, but what is money for except to make the whole world better, to help people have a better life?
— John Harvey Kellogg

William Keith became increasingly frustrated watching others outside of The San find success with their health products, while he and his brother had a winning idea waiting in the wings. Battle Creek quickly became the breakfast cereal capital of the world. People came from all around to copy The San's methods. In fact, over one hundred new cereal companies had opened in Battle Creek by the year 1912. The competition would come and go over the years, as many of the companies were unsuccessful and their product was often of poor quality compared to the big names like Kellogg and Post.

William Keith reached a point where he was fed up with his brother and was finally going to strike out on his own, but the tragic events of 1902 put his plans on hold. The main building of The San burned to the ground. William couldn't leave his brother in his time of need and Dr Kellogg quickly made plans to rebuild his beloved Battle Creek Sanitarium, bigger and better than before. William Keith stayed on during the reconstruction to be of assistance. He remained at The San for a while, but eventually put his plans into motion and went into business for himself, leaving John Harvey to his obsessions.

In 1906, William Keith made his move and finally added sugar to the breakfast flakes to help improve the taste and appeal of the product. This move was seen as a terrible sin in the eyes of John Harvey. It was the same year that William Keith founded the *Battle Creek Toasted Corn Flake Company*, while John Harvey continued to sell the cereal strictly through the Sanitarium.

John Harvey was very upset about what he saw as the commercialisation of their good family name and a product that had been intended only as a vital part of his life's work. William Keith was quickly becoming the head of a million dollar a year business and John Harvey's mood towards his little brother continued to darken over the next few years, as their relationship grew sour.

In 1910 John Harvey decided to change the name of his own company at The San to the *Kellogg Food Company*. William Keith saw this as a move of aggression and fired back by re-naming his company the *Kellogg Toasted Corn Flake Company*. William began to include his signature on every box of cereal, along with the slogan 'Beware of imitations, none genuine without this signature.'

The familial disagreement officially went to court in 1910 when William Keith sued John Harvey; John Harvey fought back by suing William Keith over the use of the family name. Dr Kellogg felt that he himself had made the Kellogg's brand name a household icon with a fine reputation, which only he could be entrusted with. The Michigan Supreme Court finally granted William Keith Kellogg the right to use his own name in his business ventures in 1920. William was a progressive businessman who ran his cereal plant on four six-hour shifts, which provided more jobs for the local economy in Detroit.

William Keith also took a page out of Post's book and would eventually start getting serious about developing more innovative ways to promote his product. Advertisements for Kellogg's would become a prevalent part of magazines, newspapers and billboards throughout the next few decades. There were a variety of marketing campaigns, such as the one for Kellogg's Bran advertisement that touted that it 'Will sweep Constipation out of your system Permanently'. Yet another example was a giant 50ft billboard in New York City's Times Square that read simply: 'I want Kellogg's'.

One of the more genius marketing campaigns that Kellogg's Cereal would offer was the 'Give your grocer a wink and see what you get' promotion. The adverts would advise shoppers to wink at their grocer and they would subsequently be given a free sample of Kellogg's Corn Flakes! The promotion went to great lengths to boost the visibility and popularity of the brand at the time.

Later in Life

The controversial doctor would continue his curious proclivities later in life. In 1906, long before the trend became infamous in Hitler's Nazi Germany, John Harvey Kellogg was an ardent eugenicist. The complicated, but disturbing, trend of eugenics in the early twentieth century often involved blatant bigotry and racism. John Harvey co-established and helped to fund the 'Race Betterment Foundation' in Battle Creek. The foundation of the racist group was to promote a purity of breeding. In fact, Kellogg himself purported that they should create a registry that would identify appropriate breeding pairs, exercising control over the white race and keeping it pure. He firmly believed in racial segregation. They also believed that anyone that wasn't of 'good stock' shouldn't breed, from the mentally ill to criminals. There were many famous eugenicists in the era, including President Theodore Roosevelt, Winston Churchill and (quite ironically) Helen Keller.

Dr Kellogg's beloved San would fall into difficult times during The Great Depression. The well-to-do business saw a drop in turnover by a devastating seventy-five per cent. In 1930 Dr Kellogg broke with the church and left The San. The Sanitarium was over three million dollars in debt by the middle of the 1930s and in 1933, it fell into receivership. Kellogg left Michigan and established a new life in Florida with an interest in opening another Sanitarium there. William Keith made his brother the generous offer of 1.5 million dollars (around 21 million dollars today) to purchase the Battle Creek Food Company. John Harvey was insulted by the offer, feeling that it was far too low. Dr Kellogg continued working in medicine, as a pioneer in recognising the risks of high blood pressure and heart disease. It was during his time in Florida that his relevance began to fade, as medicine continued to grow and progress beyond his out-dated ideals.

The Death of Dr Kellogg

In October of 1942 William Keith Kellogg made a tepid journey down to the state of Florida, where his brother John was residing, to discuss some business concerns. William Keith arrived expecting their usual confrontational relationship, only to find that John Harvey had been rapidly losing touch with reality. William Keith found his brother rambling and confused, a shell of the once sharp and decisive man. The divide that was caused by the Kellogg brothers' cereal wars had taken a deep toll on their relationship and now that John Harvey had all but lost his senses, any hope of reconciliation was out the window. It is said that John Harvey wrote a seven-page letter of apology to William Keith on his deathbed, but his brother never received it. The Kellogg brothers would never speak to each other again. John Harvey Kellogg passed away on 14 December 1943, at the ripe old age of 91. William Keith Kellogg lived until 6 October 1951, also dying at the age of 91.

Kellogg's Cereal Today

The Kellogg brothers continued to be a stark contrast. William Keith Kellogg was not an ardent eugenicist and, by contrast, he established the W.K. Kellogg Foundation in 1930. According to the official W.K.K.F. website their mission is:

> *The W.K. Kellogg Foundation was established in 1930 by breakfast cereal pioneer W.K. Kellogg, who defined its purpose as '...administering funds for the promotion of the welfare, comfort, health, education, feeding, clothing, sheltering and safeguarding of children and youth, directly or indirectly, without regard to sex, race, creed or nationality....' To guide current and future trustees and staff, he said, 'Use the money as you please so long as it promotes the health, happiness and well-being of children.'*
>
> *The foundation receives its income primarily from the W.K. Kellogg Foundation Trust, which was set up by Mr Kellogg. In addition to its diversified portfolio, the trust continues to own substantial equity in the Kellogg Company. While the company and the foundation have enjoyed a long-standing relationship, the foundation is governed by its own independent board of trustees. The foundation receives its income primarily from the trust's investments.*
>
> *Over the years, the Kellogg Foundation's programming has continued to evolve, striving to remain innovative and responsive to the ever-changing needs of society. Today, the organisation ranks among the world's largest private foundations, awarding grants in the United States, Mexico, Haiti, northeastern Brazil and southern Africa.*

Chapter Eight

Winchester: Guns to Ghosts

T he twisted tale of the Winchester Mystery House is one of California's most enduring legends. A spooky and supernatural tale follows the legacy of the late Sarah Winchester and the seemingly bizarre home that the wealthy gun heiress built to appease the angry spirits of the dead. It is said that the spirits haunted her due to her departed husband's work in manufacturing firearms during the Civil War era and beyond. If you believe the inflated campfire tales, the grieving widow turned to a medium in the height of her misery and regularly held séances to communicate with the 'other side', all while building a home that featured staircases to nowhere and closed-off hallways. The truth behind the legend may be infinitely less spectacular, but equally as tragic.

The Winchester Rifle

This chapter focuses on the legacy of the tortured widow, Sarah Winchester, but in order to understand her pain and paranoia it is important to understand the legacy of death and pain that lead to the Winchester curse. There are iconic images of the Wild West, the cowboy with his trademark hat and, of course, his Winchester rifle. The imagery of legendary characters, like Buffalo Bill Cody and Annie Oakley, can be seen brandishing the rifle in pictures of the era. In fact, the only picture known to exist of the infamous outlaw Billy the Kid shows him posing proudly with his Winchester model 1873 rifle. The iconic weapon also became a staple in Hollywood westerns, with John Wayne himself using them in some of his more famous films, like *True Grit* and *Stagecoach*. Don't mistake the Winchester firearms for harmless movie props, the guns remain a piece of history and culture for a reason, they were as deadly a weapon as the world had seen to that point. The gun emerged at just the right time to change history, and would be dubbed: 'The gun that won the west'.

The expansion of the American settlers westward was a major catalyst in United States history. The establishing of cities and towns all across the country and the eventual creation of the railroad to unite the east and west serve as turning points in history. The 1850s were a treacherous time to travel across the country. Pioneers left the comforts of home behind to make their way across America and build a new life in a gritty and unfamiliar area. This is an era before automobiles and before the mid-western territories were settled, so dangers abounded. The terrain and elements were harsh enough, but there were also aggressions with the Native Americans, who were none too happy to find people trudging across the country into their territories and claiming land as their own. The only real method of defence that a pioneer and his family would have on a wagon train is a single shot rifle. It was a step up from the musket, but not by much. It took an experienced user approximately ten seconds to reload the rifle after each shot, leaving them vulnerable during that time. It has been suggested that without the innovations of Winchester's firearms, the west may never have been settled at all.

The man who would come to revolutionise firearms and have his name emblazoned in history and forever tied with armaments, was as far from being a gun maker as it is possible to imagine. Oliver Fisher Winchester was born on 30 November 1810 to Samuel and Hannah Winchester. When Oliver was a boy he worked on a farm and attended school during the winter when the farm work was on hold. Oliver Winchester began his life in the carpentry trade, working as an apprentice throughout his teenage years, and soon moved to Baltimore to oversee the production of various buildings and homes. Despite starting a business being a risky venture in the economic climate of 1837, Winchester made the bold move of opening his own men's clothing store. Winchester became a producer of men's shirts and found a moderate level of success. In 1847, he sold his store in Baltimore and moved to New Haven, Connecticut, where he would stay for the remainder of his days. Winchester had a unique idea for improving upon the method of shirt making by inventing a curved seam, which would remedy the pull on the neckband, causing wear on the garments. His patent, number 5,421, was granted on 1 February 1848.

Winchester was anxious to go to work, but he needed a business partner to get him off the ground. He joined forces with John M. Davies to form the Winchester & Davies factory. The business would use Winchester's patented seam to produce quality men's shirts for many years. The success of the company would make Winchester a very comfortable man and by 1855 his company was grossing upwards of six hundred thousand dollars a year. Oliver was looking for other ventures to invest in so he could establish and expand his wealth. He soon found an emerging marketplace in which to invest.

On 21 August 1849 prolific inventor Walter Hunt patented a brand new invention, the repeating firearm. Hunt held patents for many items we now take for granted, such as the fountain pen, sewing machine and the safety pin. His US patent 6,663 was granted for a 'Combined piston breech and firing cock repeating gun' and US patent 5,701 for his 'Rocket Ball' ammunition. He took his patent and developed what he called the 'Volition Repeater' rifle. This revolutionary measure would pave the way for the most effective firearms of the era, but it wasn't Hunt's gun that would do the job. In fact, it suffered from numerous defects, which kept it from ever making its way to mass production. The idea was improved upon by Lewis Jennings and produced by Robbins and Lawrence. The new design produced by Jennings was awkward to hold and fire, not to mention the weak strength of the ammunition. The gun was a failure, only 1,000 units were produced before it was pulled from the market. It was at the Robbins and Lawrence factory that two gunsmiths, Horace Smith and Daniel Wesson, began developing improvements on the Jennings design.

The duo were eventually able to patent their own magazine firearm on 14 February 1854. The repeating rifle that Smith and Wesson had developed was a vast improvement on the previous Jennings model. This was the first time we saw the lever design able to swing forward, allowing for a faster repetition of firing. The image of a cowboy cocking the Winchester rifle and firing in rapid succession would be made iconic by Hollywood and in television shows like the opening to the 1958 western classic series *The Rifleman*. Guns like the Smith and Wesson rifle allowed the user to load up to thirty bullets into the magazine, which was conveniently located under the barrel of the gun. Adverts for the gun claimed that it could be loaded in less than a minute and that the ammunition was waterproof. The entire design was far more streamlined. Smith and Wesson formed their first joint venture, Smith & Wesson Company, around their new design and went forward with production. They changed the name to the Volcanic Repeating Arms Company in 1855 to mirror the name that they gave their rifle, the Volcanic.

Smith and Wesson had a gun and a venture, but now they needed to find some backers, investors who could take the production to the next level. Oliver Winchester purchased eighty shares of the upstart Volcanic Repeating Arms Company in 1855. This marked the beginning of a legacy that is still going strong today. It was a rocky start for Smith and Wesson; though we know them today as legends in the firearms business, the Volcanic Repeating Arms Company suffered from a lukewarm reception from the public. It turns out that their ammunition just wasn't powerful enough to shoot long distances, or to do enough damage, so the sales quickly began to suffer. The investors pulled out one by one, even Smith and Wesson moved on. In 1856 Winchester was the sole remaining investor, and he bought out the remains of the company for forty thousand dollars, determined to make it work. Now sitting as the president and treasurer of the Volcanic Repeating Arms Company, Oliver Winchester went to work making changes that he thought would take the business to a new level.

The first change brought about by Oliver was a name change to the New Haven Arms Company. A fresh start and a name without a stigma was necessary to try and carve out a piece of the market and convince gun dealers to carry his product. Winchester personally oversaw the factory, which employed dozens of gunsmiths and machinists. He was a shirt maker and a businessman, which set him apart from other gun makers, who were largely machinists and gunsmiths themselves. Winchester needed to bring in an expert to help him develop a more effective weapon. That man was Benjamin Tyler Henry, a masterful mechanic who Winchester had utilised to care for the 500 sewing machines in his shirt factory. In 1857 Henry became the plant superintendent, using the limited gunsmith experience that he had picked-up as a teenager. What he lacked in experience, Henry made-up for in dedication. It is said that he lived in the factory, sleeping only a few hours at a time, working tirelessly on a new rifle design.

It was around this time that the American Civil War was beginning to brew. The North and South were at odds and by this time, their new gun design, the 'Henry rifle', went into production. The Henry rifle also included a brand new innovation, metallic cartridges to house the ammunition. The idea of metal bullets is still the industry standard today, but back then it was a radical concept, which created waterproof ammunition that was easier to store and carry. The Henry rifle was available to the public by 1862 and the Civil War had been raging on since the previous year. The demand for weaponry was high, but the federal government was hesitant to commit to the weapon in any major way, largely due to the unique ammunition that was required. The government was also unsure of how well the rifle would perform on the battlefield and how reliable it would be. In the past, so many models had disappointed, and it was hardly the time to chance everything on a new product.

Never one to miss a promotional opportunity, Winchester sent a special Henry rifle to President Lincoln. The rifle was the sixth 'Henry' ever produced and was plated in gold and intricately inscribed and personalised. Rifles were also sent to Secretary of War, Edwin McMasters Stanton, and Secretary of the Navy, Gideon Welles. In fact, it is a long-standing tradition that every standing President of the United States since has been presented with their own Winchester rifle. Despite these efforts, Winchester was only able to sell 1,731 models of the Henry rifle to the Union army. That's not to say that the rifle wasn't more heavily used by the soldiers of the North, but the capital for those guns had to come out of their own pockets. Word of mouth about the reliability and rapid-fire capability of the Henry rifle travelled fast through the ranks of the Union army, and soon soldiers who were earning limited incomes of around $13 a month were happy to spend their precious little money to purchase the $50 rifle. They would carry the weapon and purchase the ammunition on their own, anything to help better ensure a safe return home. The Henry rifle could be fired fourteen to fifteen times per minute, so a Union soldier would naturally want to take that into war against the Confederate soldiers, who were still often firing single-shot muskets. It is estimated that somewhere between six and seven thousand soldiers carried the Henry rifle into combat throughout the Civil War.

Winchester's Henry rifle would prove itself during the Civil War, but it was during the westward migration of America that Winchester firearms would truly shine. In 1865 Oliver renamed his company the Winchester Arms Company, after a short stint as the Henry Repeating Rifle Company. The sales of the Henry rifle grew strong once the rifle had proven its worth, with sales reaching 13,000 units. The Henry was a great gun, but it had a few faults that Winchester wanted to improve upon. The barrel would often become hot enough to burn the user when the rifle had been fired in rapid succession. Also, the exposed magazine would allow dirt to clog the weapon and the ammunition wasn't powerful enough for big game or long-range shooting. Winchester brought in a new superintendent for his factory, Nelson King, who would solve these defects by developing the Winchester Model 1866 rifle. The sales for the Model 1866 would skyrocket the company to success, selling over 170,000 units. The gun, dubbed the 'Yellow Boy' by the Native Americans due to its brass features, found fame during the 1876 Battle of Little Big Horn, also known as 'Custer's Last Stand'. The infamous battle-turned-massacre was largely a case of the American soldiers being outgunned by the combined force of the Lakota Sioux, Arapaho and Northern Cheyenne tribes. The United States 7th Cavalry was still armed with single shot weapons, despite the lessons learned during the Civil War. The Native American forces were, by contrast, armed with Winchester repeating rifles. To cut a long story short, the result was an overwhelming defeat of the Cavalry by the Native Americans; so devastating that it made the history books.

In 1873 Winchester released yet another rifle and this one was far more powerful. The Winchester Model 1873 saw the frame of the rifle change from brass to iron, and the addition of removable side panels, which made the gun easier to maintain without a complete disassembly. The ammunition was also far more powerful, with a revolutionary central fire round that included ⅓ more black powder. The amped-up ammunition allowed the gun to bring down a buffalo from 200yds away. The new gun was widely adopted by lawmen, in fact the Texas Rangers, who had previously used the Winchester Model 1866, upgraded to the new rifle and used it well into the twentieth century. President Theodore Roosevelt, who was an avid hunter, touted the Model 1873 as one of his favourite weapons in his memoirs.

The Winchester rifles continued production long after the west was won, and carved out a status as a cultural icon, as the weapon of choice for cowboys, ranchers, outlaws and lawmen. Despite the high level of success that their business ventures came to enjoy, the Winchester family seemed to have a bit of a curse in play. Oliver passed away on 11 December 1880, at the age of 70. He passed ownership of the company over to his son William, who would die only a few months later of tuberculosis, leaving behind a devastated and distraught widow Sarah, who would cast a dark cloud over the Winchester family name, one that lives on in legend to this day.

Sarah Winchester's Early Life

The exact date that Sarah Lockwood Pardee was born remains shrouded in mystery, much like the confusing legacy she left in her wake. What we do know is that she was born sometime around the year 1840 in New Haven, Connecticut, to Leonard and Sarah Pardee. It wasn't until she met William Winchester, the son of Oliver Winchester, in her early twenties that Sarah's life would become of public interest and be far more closely documented. William and Sarah married on 30 September 1862

The newlywed couple moved to a large stone house on Prospect Street in New Haven, very close to the Winchester factories. This was during the turbulent era of the Civil War (1861-1865). From the balcony on the back of her home, Sarah could see the factories where the arms were made. The war kept William quite busy with the Winchester Repeating Arms business and Sarah longed for the end of the war, because she understandably wanted more time with her new husband. The couple would have one child, a little girl named Annie Pardee Winchester, born on 15 June 1866. Tragically, baby Annie would only live a short time, dying on 24 July 1866.

The day that Annie was laid to rest, it is said that a terrible storm raged, complete with a dramatic tinge of thunder and lightning, as though Sarah's emotions could almost govern the weather. Her grave read simply 'Babie Annie' and now lies next to her two parents in Evergreen Cemetery. Sarah and William's infant daughter died of a condition known as marasmus, which was untreatable at the time. Modern medicine now associates marasmus with a protein deficiency known as kwashiorkor.

Tragedy would again strike the Winchester household fifteen years later, when William began to show signs of illness. He was working hard, nearly around the clock, so Sarah could have assumed that exhaustion and stress played a role in his wellbeing, but there was more to it than that. It took years of slowly wasting away, but William fell seriously ill and died on 7 March 1881. The legend goes that on the day of his funeral, there was thunder and lightning in the sky yet again.

Sarah was left alone in a large, cold, dark home overlooking the Winchester factories where her husband spent a good portion of their married life, and which she may very well have blamed for his eventual death. They stood like grisly beacons, continuing to make instruments of death on a daily basis. Sarah Winchester would be the sole heiress to her husband's full estate, a fact that would leave her wealthy beyond the wildest dreams of most, but Sarah was so haunted by the death of her family that she couldn't enjoy it.

The legend goes that Sarah, obsessed with death and desperately seeking contact with her deceased husband, fell into company with a medium from Boston named Adam Coons. It is also said that she had an interest in the occult and believed that she could communicate with the dead through Coons. In 1884 she placed an urn on the graves of William and Annie that said: 'Hearts are dust. Heart's love remains. To live in the hearts we leave behind is not to die.'

Legend further tells us that Coons helped Sarah establish total communication with William in the afterlife. Hoping for words of love, she was disappointed by a gloomy and dark message from the tortured spirit of her husband. William's ghost told Sarah that she would be forever haunted by the spirits of those killed by the Winchester rifle. The spirits had also decreed that the Winchester family needed to provide them with a final resting place. William then told her to build a house that would never be completed, with infinite rooms that would provide shelter for the spirits. Sarah believed that by doing this she would gain immortality. This is the legend, and the basis for much of the thought about the motivations of Sarah Winchester and her 'mad' mystery home. How much of this is actually true? Surprisingly little, it turns out.

I spoke to Sarah Winchester's biographer Mary Jo Ignoffo about the reality of Sarah's life and she had a vastly different picture to paint. Mary Jo spent five years researching Sarah Winchester's life for her book *Captive of the Labyrinth: Sarah L. Winchester, Heiress to the Rifle Fortune*. Mary Jo slaved over a ton of first-hand information from sources such as letters that Sarah had exchanged with her attorney; the daybooks of her ranch foreman John Hansen; and property deeds from Santa Clara and San Mateo counties. Interestingly, when I questioned Ignoffo about Sarah's relationship with medium Adam Coons, the pivot-point for the entire legend, she informed me that in all of her research she had never been able to locate a record of a medium by that name. It wouldn't be surprising if a recently widowed woman with a fortune at her disposal was preyed upon by a number of characters looking to pedal spiritual advice for a price, but I also couldn't locate any actual evidence of one named Adam Coons.

Sarah soon travelled to Santa Clara valley in San Jose, California, where she bought forty-four acres of land and an eight room farmhouse that was under construction. It is said that the townsfolk watched in awe as Sarah brought many wagons of materials, at all times of day and night, to build her ambitious new home. Sarah spoke only to the architects and the carpenters on any regular basis and she was regularly dressed in black mourning clothes and a veil, which would be traditional grieving garb for the era.

The 'mystery home' of Sarah Winchester would finally settle with an astounding 160 rooms, 110 of which are currently available for the public to view on regular tours that are still held there. The house is an Eastlake shingle Queen Anne design that would end up costing Sarah more than five million dollars to construct. The building work wouldn't actually end until Sarah's death on 5 September 1922.

The crews of carpenters and masons worked day and night for several years. After a time, Sarah fired her architect, because she wanted to be fully in charge of providing the designs. The home looked like a typical Victorian mansion from the outside and fit well into the landscape of the town, but much to the surprise of the locals, it continued to expand and grow beyond expectations. Keeping in mind that no one in the local community had any idea about Sarah's supposed premonitions, they only knew what they saw from a distance. The casual passers-by could see Mrs Winchester, still in mourning, lurking around the extensive grounds, but they say that she never acknowledged or spoke to anyone on the outside. She remained an enigma, keeping fairly secluded, not socialising much with the locals.

Mary Jo Ignoffo also provided some insight into how Sarah was perceived by the local San Jose community: 'At the time, Sarah Winchester was perceived as building an excessively large and decorous house and as not 'going in' with the neighbors (quote from newspaper). A few very close neighbors visited her property and occasionally did favors for her.'

Sarah may have been in deep mourning and isolation, but she did enjoy the inheritance worth nearly twenty million dollars, plus an income from the Winchester Repeating Rifle Company profits that would equal around $1,000 per day. Cost was clearly not an issue for Sarah and her bizarre home renovations reflect that fact.

The former workmen from the home would spread stories and rumours about what they saw while in the home, to the eager ears of the local townies. The interior of the home was a mysterious labyrinth of mazes. There were passageways connecting many of the rooms, which Sarah would use on a regular basis to move around the home unbeknownst to the staff. There were stray hallways and corridors that led nowhere. It is said that the layout was so unnerving that new servants didn't like to stray from the known hallways. There is one particular seven-story staircase that was 9ft tall and had forty steps, each of those steps being only 2ins in height. This oddity is likely due to the severe arthritis that Sarah suffered from.

By the turn of the century, the house engulfed the outbuildings and stables on the land and any others were soon gone. All of the original eight rooms of the house had disappeared. She had to add a high fence to keep people out who came to get a look at her and the house. She even planted a high cypress hedge and hired gardeners to focus on the hedge to nurture it into a thick green wall to keep away prying eyes. Any request to see her or her servants was refused.

In 1904 Sarah had withdrawn from society so completely that she could no longer deal with the servants or workmen anymore. Sarah's niece Margaret Merriam soon moved in to assist as a liaison to all people. No one was allowed to see Sarah anymore without her full veils and mourning garb and they certainly weren't allowed to communicate with her directly. The butler would see her in a more relaxed state, only because he had access to her for the purpose of serving her meals.

The seven-story house soon became somewhat of an attraction that drew visitors from miles around. Sarah had a particular obsession with the number thirteen. One press release from the 'Winchester Mystery House' details her preoccupation: 'Her will had 13 parts and was signed 13 times. The house has 13 bathrooms, and the 13th bathroom has 13 windows and

13 steps leading to it. Many windows have 13 panes and rooms have 13 ceiling panels.' The peculiar mansion spans 24,000sq ft of space and boasts 2,000 doors, fifty-two skylights, forty bedrooms, three elevators, two basements, six kitchens, thirteen bathrooms, forty staircases, forty-seven fireplaces and ten thousand windows.

It is said that the turnaround was high amongst the servants. The legends say that the servants would sometimes leave out of intense fear, and sometimes they were fired for prying or defying orders. Eventually a regular staff was established who would stay with Sarah and protect her from the prying, hurtful eyes of the outside world. The wall of secrecy surrounding the widow and her house only continued to grow as the years went by.

Mrs Winchester would use her secret séance room on a regular basis, but she was so suspicious of prying eyes that she would take a variety of different corridors and secret passageways to the room each time she used it. The séance room was a small, blue room with a barred window and only one obvious entrance and exit. The secret exit did exist, but it was carefully hidden inside a closet. Sarah would spend hours in the room, hoping to consult the spirit of her dearly departed husband. Servants are said to have been able to hear, from outside the door, her speaking out loud to him during these sessions. There were many legends surrounding these supernatural sessions, mostly purported by ex-staff members and local gossips. One such tale spun the yarn that the servants could hear a baby crying from within the room, and another instance entailed a servant who hid in the room. She claims to have seen an ethereal and mystic hand appear out of nowhere with an ornate chalice that Mrs Winchester subsequently drank from in some sort of bizarre ritual. These claims, however, remain absolutely unsubstantiated gossip and urban legend.

Another legend states that Sarah had announced to her servants one day that she would be hosting a lavish ball that very evening, seemingly out of nowhere. A new ballroom had just been completed in the home, with a gorgeous Tiffany chandelier, and she intended to host a celebration ball with food and rare wines. A troupe of musicians were hired and brought in that night to entertain and delight the partygoers with song. A luxurious and decadent dinner was also served on beautifully decorated buffet tables. The ball began with all the appropriate fare, including the butler announcing the names of guests as they arrived. The band is said to have looked on, confused and disturbed, as people were being announced and the ball was rocking along – but there were no actual guests present. The musicians, unnerved by the entire evening, finally fled the eerie scene at two in the morning.

In the wee hours of 18 April 1906, the massive San Andreas fault began to rumble and groan. The subsequent earthquake caused immense damage to Sarah's home and the house became a death trap with Sarah trapped alone in her room. The servants were unable to hear her muffled cries for help for several hours. They finally discovered her in the ruins of her once beautiful bedroom. The front portion of the house, an area that she had ensured was very lavish and expensive, is what sustained the majority of the damage in the earthquake. The tortured widow took the natural disaster as a sign from 'the beyond' that her decadence was being punished. New orders were given to board-up that area of the house and no one was allowed there again after that point. The quake shook Sarah so deeply that she left the home to live in various other places. One such place was a houseboat anchored in the San Francisco Bay. Other sites included a ranch, and a home in Atherton. Sarah continued to move around for the next six years. She would send daily orders to the foreman, and construction crews would continue, but she did not return to the home once during this time.

In the spring of 1912, Sarah returned to the home and renewed the building at a near frantic pace. She was suffering from a crippling form of arthritis and her health was beginning to decline. Thanks to her condition she was often confined to her living quarters. A decade later on, the night of 4 September 1922, the evening crew stopped work to play cards and have some whiskey to relax and unwind after a hard day's work. They hadn't seen Mrs Winchester for months and weren't sure if she was even still on the grounds, or living in her other home. The following morning, Sarah's niece Margaret went to her room in order to check on her aunt. The tortured widow Sarah Winchester was dead; she had died in her sleep.

The obituary in one San Jose newspaper recalled the widow's life: 'She has lived a quiet, secluded life here for about thirty years. For many years she has aided financially the department of the Connecticut state hospital devoted to the treatment of tuberculosis patients, as well as being interested in other charitable activities.' Sarah Winchester may have been laid to rest, but her legend had only just begun.

The Winchester Legacy

The beautiful and carefully restored Queen Anne Victorian home at 525 S. Winchester Boulevard still stands today. Today, the six-acre property is a tourist trap. You can visit the home and take tours that include the grand ballroom, private séance chambers and more – there is even a special 'behind the scenes' tour. The tour guides will tell tales of the mysterious widow who spent her millions on a home to house the spirits that haunted her.

During the Halloween season tour guides now offer a night-time 'Halloween Candlelight Tour' at the home, promoting the supernatural aspects of the legend of Sarah Winchester's Mystery House. The press release for the tour touts it as a seriously spooky event:

> *TIME magazine has called us one of the 'Most Haunted Places in the World' and this Halloween we're enhancing what's already here with an all-new macabre, atmospheric, and truly creepy overlay with our limited time only Halloween Candlelight Tour offering.*

Peter Overstreet, one of the successful directors at the Great Dickens Christmas Fair in San Francisco states:

> *During the candlelit visit some kind of paranormal force will definitely be awakened within the house, much to the shock of guests on the tour … . This all-new experience for guests to the Winchester Mystery House will be both a physical visit and a great example of 'theater of the mind' where your imagination is coerced to fill in the blanks to even more frightful effect.*

It is commonly thought that after a certain point, Sarah's isolation may have had a lot to do with her severe arthritis. In reality, she was an intelligent, generous woman who spoke four languages, loved the arts, sent gifts of food from her garden to needy families and, according to her former servants, donated to many charities. The facts surrounding the mysterious widow are actually few and far between. Her legacy is shrouded in legend and hearsay, which all serves to make her life seem far more fanciful and mysterious than it likely was. Mary Jo Ignoffo described Sarah Winchester to me as:

> *… a brilliant investor, more talented than her peers, male or female; with investments in land, fruit, stocks, bonds. She would not have called herself a feminist or an icon. She wanted to be a talented architect, but she believed the results of the earthquake highlighted her shortcomings in that pursuit. She did not believe in inherited wealth, and so she sought to make her money grow. I think she is far more interesting and believable as a three-dimensional historical figure – someone who faced many challenges in life and found very creative and effective ways to*

deal with them. To me, it is far more intriguing to understand that, for a dozen years or more, she got up everyday and managed a major construction project – not for some fanciful reason about obsession or ghosts, but because it was a creative outlet and she preferred a life of work rather than leisure. She was a busy woman, right up to the end.

When it comes to the question of her supposed obsession with the occult, Mary Jo takes umbrage with the status quo. 'I found no historical evidence that Sarah Winchester was obsessed. She could have joined a local group that routinely held séances, and she did not. As for the occult, she belonged to an Episcopalian church.'

When they removed Sarah's remaining personal items from the home, a small box was recovered that consisted of some of her dear husband's items and a small lock of blonde hair from her baby. We should perhaps focus on remembering Sarah not as an isolated and superstitious eccentric, but as a devoted wife and mother who was tragically stripped of everything she knew and loved. Sarah Winchester was left with a hollow fortune and, instead of bringing her comfort and distraction, it served only to further drive her intense amount of sorrow and grief. Her elaborate and mysterious home was simply her best way of honouring the memory of her loved ones.

The Winchester Mystery House Today

The Winchester mansion boasted one hundred and sixty rooms...or so we thought. During the writing of this book a secret attic room was uncovered by those who run the mansion. The preservation team at the house were able to recover several items from the room, from a Victorian couch, sewing machine, and pump organ, to paintings and a dress form. The room was boarded up after the 1906 earthquake and had not seen the light of day until now. The mansion remains a landmark for both California and San Jose and is even listed in the National Archive of Historic Places.

Chapter Nine

Bakelite: Killer Plastic

Bakelite was one of the more fascinating of the early developments in plastic and, although it was only on the market for a relatively short time, it was utilised during the glamorous era of the Roaring Twenties on many beautiful products, making it very collectible still today. It was ultimately fatal controversy involving the family who invented this amazing product that clings to the memory, and continues to fascinate as one of the more salacious dramas in recent brand history.

A Brief History of Plastics

Plastics are one of the most revolutionary and important inventions to come out of the nineteenth century. Plastics can be tough and rigid, soft and flexible, transparent or opaque. Plastic began to be mass manufactured just over a century ago, which makes it a very modern material. Prior to the inception of plastics, other similar materials such as shell and horn were often used. By 1725, London had become the major European centre for the moulding of horn. By the nineteenth century the common use of ivory and tortoise shell was no longer viable because the natural resources needed to poach the animal materials were being over-farmed and were becoming scarce. There was a great need for an artificial material to take their place, and that is where plastic came into play.

The first plastic was introduced at the Great International Exhibition in London in 1862. This is where British chemist Alexander Parkes introduced the world to his invention, Parkesine. The product resembled the look of ivory and horn and seemed like a great new alternative. The reasons for the failure of the product vary, depending on the source. There are some who say that it wasn't a viable option thanks to inflated production costs, and others who attest that Parkes used inferior materials, thus producing inferior products that weren't well received by consumers. Regardless of the reasoning, Parkesine was a commercial failure, but soon another innovation in plastics would emerge to take its place.

Inventor John Wesley Hyatt, Jr. and his older brother Isaiah, both moved to the bustling and busy city of Chicago early in their adult lives. John worked as a printer's apprentice and began inventing at a young age, while Isaiah was a newspaper editor. The Hyatt brothers filed for their very first patent on 19 February 1861 under Patent 31,461. The invention was an 'Improved Knife-Sharpener'. The Hyatt brothers seemed to work well together and would continue to do so in the future, leading up to their most important discovery. The two would file another patent the next year, on 17 June 1862, for an 'improvement in knife or scissors sharpeners' (Patent 35,652).

In 1863, Phelan & Collender, the largest billiard supply company in the United States, were running a contest, seeking a synthetic replacement material to the ivory billiard balls that had long been the industry standard. The material was beginning to show signs of scarcity, due to the over-farming of elephant tusks. The hefty bounty of $10,000 was offered to anyone who could bring the company a new synthetic. John Wesley Hyatt, Jr. was one of the people that put his hat in the race, and to great success. Hyatt kept working in the print shop to pay the bills, but in his spare time at night he would work feverishly on the new invention.

In 1865 Hyatt was successful in creating a compound that consisted of a wood fibre core covered with a shellac and ivory dust. It is unclear whether he won the contest or was awarded any of the prize money from Phelan & Collender. On 10 October 1865, John Hyatt was granted his first solo patent for 'Billiard-balls' that detailed his new method for creation (Patent 50,359). He would soon form the Hyatt Billiard Ball Company with his friend Peter Kinnear. Hyatt needed to keep experimenting and developing new incarnations of his product because, while it was a step in the right direction, it still lacked the density and characteristics of ivory in many ways. It's a good thing he still needed his day job, because it was one fateful day working in the print shop that Hyatt would discover the lead he needed to change history.

It was a spilled bottle of collodion that sparked Hyatt's imagination. He went to clean up the spill, no doubt with annoyance that he would have a sticky mess on his hands, since collodion was a syrupy mixture that was used for coating photography in those days. Printers would use the substance, marketed then as 'new-skin' to coat their hands for protection while they were working. Instead of a mess he was encountered by a small amount of dried material that seemed to resemble the thickness and consistency of ivory. Collodion was, after all, primarily made of an alcohol and nitrocellulose mixture. Hyatt had exactly what he was looking for; he just needed a way to produce it effectively as a fully developed material. The experimentation began full-time, with Hyatt working with both liquid and solid collodion.

Years later, when Hyatt finally combined collodion with camphor and applied a heat to it, he discovered a mouldable, semi-synthetic thermoplastic. The Hyatt brothers wasted no time in looking after their interests and quickly filed for a patent. Patent 91,341 was granted on 15 June 1869 for an 'Improved Method Of Making Solid Collodion'. The patent explanation read:

Our invention consists of a new and improved method of manufacturing solid collodion and its compounds; its essential feature being the employment of a very small quantity of ether or other appropriate solvent, and dissolving pyroxyline therewith, under a heavy pressure, so that a comparatively hard and solid product is obtained, with great economy of solvents and saving of time.

The brothers learned, with a consultation from a chemist, that they had to be very careful to not apply too much heat to their compound, because it was highly flammable. They were also advised that dental-plate blanks and dentures might be a good marketplace for their invention. Rubber had long been used to make dentures, but the costs of rubber were rapidly increasing and that fact that their collodion concoction was clear in its original state made it perfect for adding dyes and pigments to that could match the various colours needed. There were further alterations needed to their method and, on 12 July 1870, Patent 105,338 for the 'Improvement in Treating and Molding Pyroxyline' was granted; this final version of the Hyatt brothers' plastic was dubbed 'Celluloid' by Isaiah. The brothers then established the Albany Dental Plate Company and the Celluloid dental blanks were born.

Throughout the 1870s the various applications for Celluloid began to become clear to the Hyatt brothers. They continued to improve on their manufacturing techniques and found that the clear plastic could be used to imitate a number of popular high-end materials, from amber and ivory, to coral and jet. The brothers began to manufacture a variety of products and Celluloid would come to be used for everything from vanity items to piano keys, cuffs and even glasses frames. Celluloid was a revolutionary product, but it wasn't without distinct disadvantages. The reality was that Celluloid was highly flammable and subject to premature decomposition. The plastic staple was eventually replaced by a new and exciting material dubbed Bakelite.

Early Life of Leo Baekeland

It was shortly after the turn of the twentieth century and a new product was about to be introduced to the marketplace by Belgian–American Leo Henricus Arthur Baekeland. Leo Baekeland was a chemist, born on 14 November 1863, in Ghent, Belgium. He was the son of humble parents; his mother was a housemaid and his father, a shoe mender. Baekeland was able to utilise his voracious mind and intellect to elevate himself from his meagre beginnings in Ghent. He attended the Ghent Municipal Technical School, where he graduated with honours. This achievement provided him with a scholarship to the University of Ghent in 1880, where he studied chemistry and earned a PhD by the age of 21. In 1887 Baekeland produced and patented his first invention: a process for developing photographic plates in water. He also met his future wife, Celine Swarts, while working as the associate professor of chemistry at Ghent; the couple married on 8 August 1889 and would go on to have three children: George, Nina and Jenny.

On their honeymoon, Leo and Celine took a trip to America. It wasn't just a leisure trip for the scholarly duo however; they also took the opportunity to visit a number of universities. It was a trip to Columbia University in New York City that would change Leo's fate – and the face of the plastics industry forever. It was there that he was recruited by Richard Anthony of E. & H. T. Anthony & Co., a photography company, and Professor Charles F. Chandler. Impressed with Leo's résumé to date, Anthony promptly offered him a job and tempted him and his new bride to move to America, an opportunity that they weren't about to pass up. Baekeland worked for E. & H. T. Anthony & Co. for two years, before he ventured off on his own as an independent consulting chemist. This move did not prove to be a gainful one for Baekeland and he soon turned his focus back to his inventions. Leo would go on to invent a good many items, registering over 100 patents in his lifetime. It was his boyhood interest in photography that would lead to one of his more famous inventions, and it was during this time that he produced one of his most famous products: Velox.

Due to the shaky economic climate at the end of the nineteenth century, it was difficult for an inventor to simply create a product and sell it by themselves. Baekeland was in need of financial backers. In 1891 he went into partnership with Leonard Jacob to form the Nepera Chemical Company based in the Nepera Park area of Yonkers in New York State. They began producing Velox paper by 1893 and made a significant dent in the marketplace, a dent that eventually began to affect Eastman Kodak. George

Eastman brokered a deal to purchase the company, and the patent to their Velox product, in 1899. The reports of the sum differ, but it was somewhere between seven hundred and fifty thousand and a million dollars. It is said that Baekeland himself earned two hundred and fifteen thousand dollars from the sale, an amount that would come to nearly six million dollars today. It was the money that he earned from the sale of Velox to Eastman Kodak that Baekeland would use toward creating his most lasting invention: Bakelite.

The Invention and Innovation of Bakelite

I was trying to make something really hard, but then I thought I should make something really soft instead, that could be molded into different shapes. That was how I came up with the first plastic. I called it Bakelite.

— Leo Baekeland

The road to Bakelite was paved with a few failures. The development of synthetic materials was a new venture for Baekeland, but he was unable to focus on the photography field any longer, due to a twenty-year long non-compete clause that he signed as a part of the deal with Eastman. In 1900, Leo returned to Germany to brush-up on his electrochemistry. Initially, it wasn't the intent of Baekeland to create a fully synthetic plastic; in fact he was originally looking to find a useful replacement for the commonly used material called shellac. Shellac was a resin produced from the excretion of the lac beetle, used for everything from jewellery and flooring to dentures and other moulded goods. Baekeland was successful in creating a substitute called Novolak. Leo wasn't pleased with the commercial success of the product at the time, although it is still used today, under the name Novolac, to produce everything from billiard balls to circuit boards. Novolak may not have been a success all on its own, but it would serve as the gateway, and the basis, for Bakelite.

Unsatisfied with his shellac substitute, Baekland kept experimenting with combining phenol with formaldehyde, hoping to develop a hard plastic that was mouldable. He would eventually come upon the correct process for polyoxybenzylmethylenglycolanhydride, the chemical name of Bakelite. Bakelite was often created by adding a filler, such as wood or asbestos, to the resin. The phenolic resin was such a fantastic development, not only because it was mouldable, but it was also non-flammable, unlike Celluloid. Leo applied for a patent on 13 July 1907 under the title: 'Method of making insoluble products of phenol and formaldehyde.' He also applied for patent protection around the world, in countries like Canada, Denmark, Japan, Mexico, Russia, Spain, and Hungary, to name a few. Leo Baekeland made a formal presentation at the American Chemical Society on 8 February 1909. The patent for Bakelite was finalised and officially issued on 7 December 1909, with Patent 942,699. The age of plastics had begun. In fact, the term 'plastics' was actually coined by Baekland.

In 1910, Leo Baekeland was working out of his own laboratory to produce his miracle plastic and selling enough product to justify a serious investment and expansion. He would create the General Bakelite Company, so that he could market and manufacture his product on a larger scale both in America and internationally. The then burgeoning automobile industry was one of the first major players to utilise Bakelite commercially. The resin would be used for items such as electrical and automobile insulators, because it had a fantastic resistance to heat and was itself a great electrical insulator. Bakelite would soon be used to produce everything from telephones to radios. Bakelite, and similar synthetic products, would find a lot more use during the First World War, when there wasn't time or resources to chase after the typical, naturally occurring resources.

Bakelite was marketed as 'The Material of a Thousand Uses'. The plastic was first available in clear, black, grey, blue, yellow, green, red and brown. It would be used in products ranging from kitchen utensil handles, pens, billiard balls, tobacco pipe stems, buttons, jewellery, poker chips, lamps, and even one of the original versions of the Viewmaster toy! Bakelite was extremely prevalent all over homes in both America and England. The idea of Bakelite inspired not only products, but art as well. Coco Chanel, who has her own chapter elsewhere in this book, often utilised Bakelite in her very popular jewellery throughout the 1920s. Bakelite would even be featured on the cover of the first issue of *Plastics Magazine* in October of 1925.

The marketing campaign for Bakelite touted the product as 'Helping The Family Keep Well', and pushed the various medical applications for the product. The advert highlighted the fact that Bakelite could be found in everything from hearing aids, oralights and dental restoration. The ads also implored the manufacturing industry to be open to the possibility of Bakelite: 'All major industries are making profitable use of one or more Bakelite materials, either through using them in the product itself, in production machinery, or in maintenance.'

Baekeland had managed to create a product that revolutionised the marketplace, but his patent would only last for so long – the patent for

Bakelite expired in 1927. That left the market open for other companies to swoop in and start developing their own versions of the plastic. The most famous of these was the American Catalin Corporation, which produced Bakelite-style plastic in a wider-range of colours, offering upwards of fifteen brighter colours to the public. This flooded the marketplace with a plethora of products similar to, and often mistaken for, the actual brand name Bakelite. The opening of the market didn't hurt Baekeland's business, though. In fact, in 1929, General Bakelite Company got its largest ever order from Siemens telephone for phenolic moulding powder, used for the casing of telephones.

Baekeland sold his company in 1939 and retired to spend his remaining days sailing on his yacht and enjoying the later years of his life. Leo Baekeland would go on to be renowned in his field and made the cover of the prestigious *Time Magazine* on 20 May 20 1940, wherein he was labelled as the 'Father of Plastics'. Leo Baekeland passed away on 23 February 1944, at the age of 80. The National Inventors Hall of Fame recognised Baekeland in 1978, and the Rail of Fame for United States Business Leadership would also award him posthumous honours in 1983.

The Baekeland Family

Leo Baekeland forged an amazing legacy for his family, but it was that family who would end up casting a shadow on the Bakelite legacy forever. A sad reality is that, while Leo may have worked hard for his money, inherited wealth can often end up being as much of a curse as it is a blessing. The Baekeland family fortune created a life of luxury for the next few generations, providing every comfort and advantage that wealth could buy.

Leo and Celine had had three children, but only two would survive to adulthood, George and Nina. Their daughter Jenny died at the age of 5, stricken with influenza. It was George Washington Baekeland, or rather his son and grandson, who would sully the family name forever. George and his wife Cornelia Fitch Middlebrook had two children: Cornelia Fitch 'Dickie' Baekland and Brooks Baekland. Now, by the time the grandchildren of Leo Baekeland arrived in the family, their wealth and prestige had been well established. Those that knew Brooks would describe him as arrogant and cocky, as many socialites who are born into money tend to be. Brooks fancied himself a writer, although he neglected to write much of anything at all.

Brooks's sister Cornelia introduced him to Barbara Daly, the woman he would subsequently marry. Barbara was an aspiring actress who didn't really act, just as Brooks was a writer who didn't really write. Barbara was undeniably a stunning beauty with ravishing red hair. She did model for a time, with her pictures gracing the pages of magazines like *Vogue* and *Harper's Bazaar*. The two indulged together in the never-ending sloth and decadence of a wealthy lifestyle. They would rub elbows and party with the finest in celebrity, aristocracy and the privileged all over the world. Barbara soon found herself pregnant and the couple's son, Antony, was born in August of 1946. The couple set up a more permanent home in the Upper East Side of New York City.

It is said, through gossip and various second-hand accounts, that Barbara Baekeland was infamous for her mood swings and erratic behaviour. She and Brooks entertained their scores of famous and wealthy friends in New York, including the likes of Greta Garbo and Tennessee Williams. Barbara is said to have been a heavy drinker, an ailment that didn't serve to help her already often severe depression. The marriage between her and Brooks was far from conventional as there are many accounts of regular extra-marital affairs on both sides. The overall atmosphere of hedonism and extravagance may have shielded Barbara, and ultimately her son Antony, from any outside recognition of harmful mental illness. In fact, many could easily write off Barbara's often rude and over-the-top behaviour as that of the spoiled bourgeoisie. It became increasingly clear, however, that there was more going on in the Baekeland bloodline than simple misbehaviour.

Over the course of their marriage, Brooks continued his affairs and would often raise the subject of divorce with Barbara, to which she would respond with threats or suicide attempts. The extreme tactics always worked on Brooks and he would remain in the 'marriage'. The family, along with Antony, began to move around in 1954, living in Italy, Paris and London. Barbara and Brooks shipped Antony off to boarding school when he was a young boy, not an uncommon practice for the well-to-do. Antony had a difficult time focusing in school and began to get kicked out for his poor grades; eventually he would simply leave the schools on his own and head home to his mother. Antony would end up spending a lot of time away at various boarding schools and it was during this time that the Baekelands would discover that their son was homosexual, a fact that didn't sit well with either Brooks or Barbara. The couple finally divorced in 1968, leaving Barbara alone to her own devices.

Barbara and Antony's relationship became seriously clingy and dark. Barbara was obsessed with her son's sexuality and it is said that she made many efforts to try and 'cure' her son of his homosexuality. Claims that she hired female prostitutes to take him to bed aren't difficult to find, but it is the next step that brings a truly disturbing turn to the story. Barbara was so determined to control Antony's sexuality that she allegedly engaged in an incestuous relationship with him.

There was a lot of trouble brewing for the Baekeland family, even aside from the complexities of the alleged incest. Antony was clearly mentally ill and was prone to violent outbursts. It is said that Antony would often fight with his mother and that knives were involved, but nothing serious came of it…until it did. There were some early indicators that Barbara's family may have had a history of mental illness. Although undiagnosed, we know that her mother, Nina Daly, suffered from a mental breakdown before Barbara was born and her father, Frank Daly, killed himself in 1936, when Barbara was 10 years old. Antony was in serious need of psychiatric attention, but his father refused to pay for the treatment, referring to the mental health field as 'professionally amoral'.

The violence between Antony and his mother first became a serious issue one afternoon in London in July of 1972. A violent scene unfolded that involved Antony dragging his mother by her hair and attempting to throw her into oncoming traffic. Fortunately for Barbara, her friend Susan Guinness witnessed the attack and intervened to assist her. Barbara refused to press formal charges against Antony, despite the desire of the police at the time to arrest him for attempted murder.

Antony was admitted to the Priory psychiatric hospital after the attack, but the stay was short lived. Antony had finally seen a psychiatrist for a time after the stay, despite his father's feelings on the subject. Brooks was very far removed from the lives of his ex-wife and son by this point, focusing instead on his own gallivanting. It was Antony's psychiatrist who provided Barbara with a prophetic warning on 30 October 1972. Apparently, this doctor told her bluntly that Antony was likely to kill her. It was a warning that she would fatally ignore.

The events of 17 November 1972 would go down in history. Barbara, now age 50, was at home in her penthouse apartment in London. Antony went to the apartment with a plan, one that he had been formulating in his paranoid and delusional mind for some time. He took a kitchen knife and stabbed his mother, killing her almost instantly. When the police arrived on the scene, the 25-year-old Antony was on the phone attempting to order Chinese takeaway.

Antony was institutionalised at Broadmoor Hospital in Berkshire for eight years, until his eventual release on 21 July 1980. There are some reports that say a bureaucratic mistake allowed for Antony's release from the well-known high-security psychiatric hospital. There are other accounts that claim wealthy and influential friends or family may have secured his release. The move was a tragic mistake, no matter which version of events was true.

Upon his release from Broadmoor, Antony went to New York to live with his maternal grandmother, Nina Daly. This arrangement would be short lived. It took a mere six days from Antony's release for him to become violent again; this time he attacked his elderly grandmother. He stabbed her eight times and broke some of her bones – but she did survive the attack. He later gave his reasoning behind the attack, explaining that his grandmother had been nagging him, just like his mother would. Antony was promptly arrested and sent to Rikers Island, the primary jail complex for New York City. The massive complex features both correctional and mental institutions.

On 21 March 1981, Antony appeared in court, in relation to the attack on his grandmother. The proceedings didn't go as Antony was hoping and he was said to have been distraught. He returned to his incarceration on Rikers Island at 3.30 PM, where he suffocated himself to death with a plastic bag. His body was discovered in his cell half an hour later.

Baketlite Today

The various products that were produced with Bakelite have become increasingly collectible in the modern second-hand market. The products range from baby toys, pipes and jewellery to kitchen utensils and even firearms. People are also buying it and re-carving the Bakelite name into new items, like jewellery. The repurposing of Bakelite has become a huge fad.

Interestingly, the original colours that adorned the Bakelite product have changed, courtesy of a prolonged reaction to oxygen. A few examples include the standard brown colour morphing to a black, white appears in an amber-tone, and clear products have the appearance of apple juice. In one example, a once red, white and blue patriotic American pin is now red, yellow and black in appearance.

The family controversy, the unhealthy relationship between Barbara and Antony Baekeland, and the subsequent murder of Barbara at the hands of Antony, were chronicled in the 2007 feature film, *Savage Grace*. The independent film, starring Julianne Moore and Eddie Redmayne, was nominated for an Independent Spirit Award for Best Screenplay.

Conclusion

In spite of the bizarre and sometimes horrifying histories behind these brand names, there is no doubt that these people and their inventions changed the world. There may have been an immense amount of negative energy surrounding them early on, but there were also a lot of positive contributions to society from these flawed individuals. All people are complicated and life is rarely viewable in black and white, there is always that ever important grey area to explore.

Henry Ford, for example, may have had his share of personal flaws and upsetting viewpoints, but what he did contribute to the American economy and society cannot be overlooked. The automobile industry became the backbone of the American economy for several decades thanks to Ford. The autmobile industry today accounts for at least one of every twenty-two American jobs. The only reason that the car is a commonplace feature of American life is because of Ford. He was able to manufacture his affordable Model T and set a new standard for daily life and the future growth of dozens of American cities. The groundbreaking higher wages that Ford paid with his $5 per day initiative set a new standard for the working class and helped make factory and manufaturing work a viable career option.

Imagine the world that Chanel grew up in. She was born poor and abandoned by her father. She lacked emotional connection and faced boundless misogyny in a world where she wasn't even allowed to vote, much less become a successful entrepreneur. In the face of this adversity she was able to become successful and leave a lasting mark on fashion that survives to this day. Chanel actually created costume jewellery and made it a staple, so that women wouldn't have to own just one or two key pieces of more expensive jewelry. Instead, a woman could have the option to accessorise her daily outfits with a variety of less expensive, but still flashily appearing jewellery. Chanel also helped rid women of the burdens of elaborate clothing and even more restrictive underclothes. She found difficulty in riding horses in a skirt so, in an act of inspirational feminism, she took the pants right of a male rider and put them on herself, a move that was unheard of at the time.

It soon became fashionable for women to wear pants. Add to all that 'the little black dress', a simple but elegant staple in many wardrobes.

These are just a few examples of the immense amount of good that has come from these important fixtures in history. In today's world the art of branding has become an important staple. A brand can be anything from a certain company to an individual, like an actor or singer. The benefits of branding, as they are seen today, include the building of customer loyalty and trust, enhanced product recognition, better product positioning, successful introduction of new products and the building of brand equity. Brand equity is the idea that a brand itself, rather than any one product, can be of great value. This can lead to franchising and a far higher price tag on both stock and sale prices. A brand can also be a status symbol to many, showing that you have the coolest or latest product, regardless of the quality or effectiveness of that product.

It is important to keep those that are famous and well regarded, both in history and in today's world, off a pedestal. It is easy to glorify those that contribute to culture in a positive way, but there is an old saying about Hollywood: 'never meet your heroes'. No one is perfect and we all make mistakes in life, some bigger than others. Our imperfections are often considered to be our weaknesses, but they are also a major part of our make-up as individuals. It is my sincere hope that you take away from this book the reminder that we must never forget our history – a rule that should always be carefully regarded – lest we be doomed to repeat it. When you see these products on the shelves or in your own home it's okay to use them without guilt or negative feeling, because we all know how far away these companies are from their dark pasts. Hopefully, we can remember the history and harbour the knowlege, without taking away from the fantastic products that we're left with. You can drink that Coke or eat that delicious bowl of Corn Flakes without reproach, but certainly with some enlightening anectodes to share with those close to you.

Notes

Coca-Cola

-More of Coca-Cola, 21 June 1891
http://www.atlantareconstitution.com/1891/06/21/more-of-coca-cola

-The Great Coca Cola Trial, 7 November 2010
http://drvitelli.typepad.com/providentia/2010/11/the-great-coca-cola-trial-part-2.html

-Cocaine-Cola, 19 May 2011
http://www.snopes.com/cokelore/cocaine.asp

-Williams, M.D., Edward Huntington. Negro Cocaine 'Fiends' Are A New Southern Menace, The New York Times, 8 February 1914

-The very first Coke? It was Bordeaux mixed with cocaine... and 23 other interesting facts about the world's best-known brand, 14 January 2015
http://www.dailymail.co.uk/news/article-2910885/The-Coke-Bordeaux-mixed-cocaine-23-interesting-facts-world-s-best-known-brand.html

-King, Monroe Martin. John Stith Pemberton (1831-1888), 14 May 2004
http://www.georgiaencyclopedia.org/articles/business-economy/john-stith-pemberton-1831-1888

-Hamblin, James. Why we took Cocaine out of Soda, 31 January 2013
http://www.theatlantic.com/health/archive/2013/01/why-we-took-cocaine-out-of-soda/272694/

-Pemberton, John Stith. Encyclopaedia of World Biography. *Encyclopedia. com.* 12 October 2016, http://www.encyclopedia.com/history/encyclopedias-almanacs-transcripts-and-maps/pemberton-john-stith

-The Chronicle of Coca-Cola, Coca-Cola Company, http://www.thecoca-colacompany.com/heritage/chronicle_birth_refreshing_idea.html (February 11, 2008).

-A History of Coca-Cola, Associated Content, http://www.associatedcontent.com/article/37117/a_history_of_cocacola.html (February 11 2008).

-John Stith Pemberton, article originally published in *Business Heroes Newsletter* (July 1998), http://www.cocaine.org/coca-cola/index.html (February 11, 2008).

-May, Clifford D. How Coca-Cola Obtains Its Coca, 1 July 1988, New York Times, http://www.nytimes.com/1988/07/01/business/how-coca-cola-obtains-its-coca.html

-Adams, Mike. To this day, Coca-Cola still imports coca leaves which are used to manufacture cocaine in the United States, 9 June 2011, http://www.naturalnews.com/032658_Coca-Cola_cocaine.html

-Report of the International Opium Commission, 1 February 1909, Cornell University Library, https://archive.org/stream/cu31924032583225/cu31924032583225_djvu.txt

-Martin, Jeff. The Coca Cola History Documentary.

-Fahey, David M. Temperance Movement, 10 March 2003, http://www.georgiaencyclopedia.org/articles/history-archaeology/temperance-movement

-Candler, Asa G. A Card From Mr. Candler, 13 June 1891, http://www.atlantareconstitution.com/1891/06/13/

-The Constitution, Atlanta, GA, What's In Coca Cola?, 12 June 1891, http://www.atlantareconstitution.com/1891/06/12/

-Firedog. 'Vin Mariani: An Experience with Coca & Alcohol (ID 51792)'. Erowid.org. Jun 24, 2008. erowid.org/exp/51792

-Allen, Frederick. *Secret Formula*. New York: Harper Collins, 1994.

Henry Ford

-Ford, Henry. *The International Jew: The World's Foremost Problem*, 1920.

-Colt, Sarah. *The American Experience: Henry Ford* (PBS Documentary Film), 2013.

-Grubin, David. *The Jewish Americans*, (PBS Documentary Film), 2008.

-Chartoff, Melanie. Henry Ford's Mass Production of Hate Meets Its Match, Huffington Post, 18 February 2014. http://www.huffingtonpost.com/melanie-chartoff/henry-fords-mass-producti_b_4470542.html

-History.com. This Day In History: Henry Ford Publishes The Last Issue of the Dearborn Independent. http://www.history.com/this-day-in-history/henry-ford-publishes-the-last-issue-of-the-dearborn-independent

-History.com. This Day In History: Ford's Assembly Line Starts Rolling. http://www.history.com/this-day-in-history/fords-assembly-line-starts-rolling

-History.com. Henry Ford, http://www.history.com/topics/henry-ford

-History.com. This Day In History: Beetle Overtakes Model T As World's Best-Selling Car. http://www.history.com/this-day-in-history/beetle-overtakes-model-t-as-worlds-best-selling-car

-Jewish Virtual Libarary. Anti-Semitism in the U.S.: 'The International Jew', https://www.jewishvirtuallibrary.org/jsource/anti-semitism/ford.html

-Jewish Virtual Library. The Nazi Party: Ford Motors Report on German Subsidiary in World War II, 6 December 2001. http://www.jewishvirtuallibrary.org/jsource/Holocaust/Ford1.html

-Rare Historical Photos. Henry Ford receiving the Grand Cross of the German Eagle from Nazi officials, 1938, 20 November 2013. http://rarehistoricalphotos.com/henry-ford-grand-cross-1938/

-http://www.TheHenryFord.org, 2016.

-Taylor, Mitchell. FordModelT.net, 2011-2016. http://www.fordmodelt.net/henry-ford.htm

-Wellhell. 'I regard Henry Ford as my inspiration' - Adolph Hitler, 1931, http://www.ipernity.com/blog/246215/407138

-Dobbs, Michael. Ford and GM Scrutinised for Alleged Nazi Collaboration, 30 November 1998. http://www.washingtonpost.com/wp-srv/national/daily/nov98/nazicars30.htm

-English, Simon. Ford 'used slave labour' in Nazi German plants, 3 November 2003. http://www.telegraph.co.uk/news/worldnews/northamerica/usa/1445822/Ford-used-slave-labour-in-Nazi-German-plants.html

-Klatzkin, Shmuel. Modern Anti-Semitism: The Protocols of the Elders of Zion, 21 February 2016. http://www.myjli.com/why/index.php/2016/02/21/modern-antisemitism-the-protocols-of-the-elders-of-zion/#_ftnref6

-Rudin, James A. The dark legacy of Henry Ford's anti-Semitism, 10 October 2014, https://www.washingtonpost.com/national/religion/the-dark-legacy-of-henry-fords-anti-semitism-commentary/2014/10/10/c95b7df2-509d-11e4-877c-335b53ffe736_story.html

-*The Dearborn Independent.* Anti-Semitism-Will It Appear in the United States, 19 June 1920, http://chroniclingamerica.loc.gov/lccn/2013218776/1920-06-19/ed-1/seq-2/

-Madigan, Charles M. The Libel Case With A 6-Cent Verdict, 8 June 1997, http://articles.chicagotribune.com/1997-06-08/news/9706300080_1_henry-ford-chicago-tribune-anarchist

-Wears, Adam. Ford Did Not Invent The Assembly Line, 17 July 2013, http://knowledgenuts.com/2013/07/17/ford-did-not-invent-the-assembly-line/

-United States Holocaust Memorial Museum. Protocols of the Elders of Zion: Timeline, 2 July 2016, https://www.ushmm.org/wlc/en/article.php?ModuleId=10007244

-Animal Welfare Institute. Urban Carriage Horses: Out of Step with Responsible Horse Welfare, https://awionline.org/content/urban-carriage-horses-out-step-responsible-horse-welfare

-Aronson, Sidney R. The Automobile: Its First 100 Years Documentary

-Worstall, Tim. The Story of Henry Ford's $5 a Day Wages: It's Not What You Think, 4 March 2012, http://www.forbes.com/sites/timworstall/2012/03/04/the-story-of-henry-fords-5-a-day-wages-its-not-what-you-think/#7a8247611c96

-Gale, Thomson. Henry Ford, 2003, http://www.encyclopedia.com/people/social-sciences-and-law/business-leaders/henry-ford

-Baime, A.J. Henry Ford's reign of terror: Greed and murder in Depression-era Detroit, 1 June 2014, http://www.salon.com/2014/06/01/henry_fords_reign_of_terror_greed_and_murder_in_depression_era_detroit/

HUGO BOSS

-Walters, Guy. Shameful truth about Hugo Boss's links to the Nazis revealed: As Russell Brand is thrown out of a party for accusing fashion designer of helping Hitler, 6 September 2013, http://www.dailymail.co.uk/news/article-2413371/Shameful-truth-Hugo-Bosss-links-Nazis-revealed-As-Russell-Brand-thrown-party-accusing-fashion-designer-helping-Hitler.html

-Brand, Russell. Russell Brand and the GQ awards: 'It's amazing how absurd it seems', 13 September 2013, https://www.theguardian.com/culture/2013/sep/13/russell-brand-gq-awards-hugo-boss

-Köster, Roman. Study on the Company's Foundation, 2011, http://group.hugoboss.com/en/group/about-hugo-boss/history/

-BBC.com. Hugo Boss apology for Nazi past as book is published, 21 September 2011, http://www.bbc.com/news/world-europe-15008682

-World War II: The Postdam Declaration, 2 August 1945, http://www.jewishvirtuallibrary.org/jsource/Holocaust/potsdam.html

Adidas/Puma

-Kuhn, Robert & Thiel, Thomas. Shoes and Nazi Bazookas, The Prehistory of Adidas and Puma, 4 March 2009, http://www.spiegel.de/international/germany/shoes-and-nazi-bazookas-the-prehistory-of-adidas-and-puma-a-611400.html

-The Dassler Brothers Timeline, http://dasslerbrothers.weebly.com/

-Katherina 'Kathe' Dassler: wife of Adidas founder Adolf Dassler, 23 March 2015, http://www.theherzogenaurachstory.co.uk/KaetheDassler.htm

-Connolly, Kate. Adidas v Puma: the bitter rivalry that runs and runs, 18 October 2009, https://www.theguardian.com/sport/2009/oct/19/rivalry-between-adidas-and-puma

-Akhtar, Omar. The hatred and bitterness behind two of the world's most popular brands, 22 March 2013, http://fortune.com/2013/03/22/the-hatred-and-bitterness-behind-two-of-the-worlds-most-popular-brands/

-Tousif, Muhammad Mustafa. Adidas vs. Puma: How it all started, 14 March 2016, http://bundesligafanatic.com/adidas-vs-puma-how-it-all-started-part-1/

-Adidas x Puma Documentary Film, 2005

Coco Chanel

-Flanner, Janet. 31, Rue Cambon, 14 March 1931, http://www.newyorker.com/magazine/1931/03/14/31-rue-cambon-2

-Coco Chanel - Style Icon of the 1920s, http://www.1920s-fashion-and-music.com/Coco-Chanel.html

-1920s Fashion: Style in The Jazz Age, http://www.1920s-fashion-and-music.com/1920s-fashion.html

-Hirst, Gwendoline. Chanel Biography, http://www.ba-education.com/for/fashion/chanel.html

-Picardie, Justine. The Secret Life of Coco Chanel, 5 September 2010, http://fashion.telegraph.co.uk/article/TMG7975778/The-secret-life-of-Coco-Chanel.html

-Chanel.com, http://inside.chanel.com/en/timeline/

-Schleunes, Karl A. *The Twisted Road to Auschwitz: Nazi Policy Toward German Jews, 1933–1939*. Urbana: University of Illinois Press, 1970.

-Friedländer, Saul. *Nazi Germany and the Jews*. New York: Harper Collins, 1997.

-United States Holocaust Memorial Museum, Anti-Jewish Legislation in Prewar Germany, https://www.ushmm.org/wlc/en/article.php?ModuleId=10005681

-Ross, Kim. Coco Chanel Nazi Spy, Goal Was To Use Nazi Influence To Take Back Parfums Chanel From Jewish Company, 9 December 2014, https://thestyleofthecase.wordpress.com/tag/gabrielle-coco-chanel/

-Vaughan, Hal. Sleeping With The Enemy: Coco Chanel's Secret War, 2011.

-MessyNessy, Coco Chanel Was Definitely a Nazi, 3 April 2012, http://www.messynessychic.com/2012/04/03/coco-chanel-was-definitely-a-nazi/

-Warner, Judith. Was Coco Chanel A Nazi Agent?, 2 September 2011, http://www.nytimes.com/2011/09/04/books/review/sleeping-with-the-enemy-coco-chanels-secret-war-by-hal-vaughan-book-review.html?_r=0

-Whitelocks, Sadie. Karl Lagerfeld who? Meet the REAL men behind Chanel's $19billion fortune, 25 September 2013, http://www.dailymail.co.uk/femail/article-2432311/Karl-Lagerfeld-Meet-men-Chanels-19billion-fortune--Alain-Gerard-Wertheimer.html

-Cowell, Alan. Churchill took swipe at Jews in 1937 article, 11 March 2007, http://www.nytimes.com/2007/03/11/world/europe/11iht-winston.4873300.html?_r=2

-Grear, Kelly. Nineteenth Century French Working Women: Love, Marriage and Children, 2002, http://www.uky.edu/~popkin/frenchworker/grear.htm

-Encyclopedia Brittanica. Samur France, https://www.britannica.com/place/Saumur

-Fisher, Anita L. Women In The Middle Class In The 19th Century, http://web.clark.edu/afisher/HIST253/lecture_text/WomenMiddleClass_19c_Europe.pdf

-Branson-Harper, Simone. Coco Chanel grew up in an orphanage at Aubazine in Corrèze, France, 24 March 2015, https://www.linkedin.com/pulse/coco-chanel-grew-up-orphanage-aubazine-corr%C3%A8ze-france-branson-harper

-Murciello, Laura. Coco Chanel: Biography of the World's Most Elegant Woman, 2012.

-Fleck, Danita. Paris In The Nineteenth Century: More About the Lower Class..., http://gallery.sjsu.edu/paris/social_classes/lower/lowerclass_more.html

-Higginbotham, Peter. The Workhouse: The Story of an Institution, http://www.workhouses.org.uk/

-Jackson, Julian, The Occupation of France: Queen Mary University of London Lecture, 2013.

-Beevor, Antony. An Ugly Carnival, 4 June 2009, https://www.theguardian.com/lifeandstyle/2009/jun/05/women-victims-d-day-landings-second-world-war

-Coudere, Frederic, Ritz Paris Reopening Press Kit, 2016, http://www.ritzparis.com/sites/all/themes/ritzparis_v3/pdf/Ritz_Paris_Reopening_Press_kit_EN.pdf

-Copping, Jasper. Nazis 'offered to leave western Europe in exchange for free hand to attack USSR', 26 September 2013, http://www.telegraph.co.uk/history/10336126/Nazis-offered-to-leave-western-Europe-in-exchange-for-free-hand-to-attack-USSR.html.

-Hall, John. Coco Chanel the Nazi spy: New document reveals that fashion designer worked for Hitler's military intelligence, 2 December 2014, http://www.dailymail.co.uk/news/article-2857133/Coco-Chanel-Nazi-spy-Fashion-designer-s-role-Second-World-War-scrutiny-new-document-proves-worked-Hitler-s-military-intelligence.html.

-Chen, C. Peter. World War II Database, http://ww2db.com/.

-'Hitler Tours Paris, 1940,' EyeWitness to History, 2008, www.eyewitnesstohistory.com.

Bayer

-Edwards, Jim. Yes, Bayer Promoted Heroin for Children -- Here Are The Ads That Prove It, 17 November 2011, http://www.businessinsider.com/yes-bayer-promoted-heroin-for-children-here-are-the-ads-that-prove-it-2011-11.

-Scott, Ian. Heroin: A Hundred-Year Habit, 6 June 1998, http://www.historytoday.com/ian-scott/heroin-hundred-year-habit.

-Kick, Russ. 50 Things You're Not Supposed To Know, Disinfo, 2003.

-Bayer AG. A Journey through the History of Bayer, http://www.bayer.com/en/history.aspx.

-History.com. This Day In History: Bayer Patents Aspirin, http://www.history.com/this-day-in-history/bayer-patents-aspirin.

-Bogdanich, Walt & Koli, Eric. 2 Paths of Bayer Drug in 80's: Riskier One Steered Overseas, 22 May 2003, http://www.nytimes.com/2003/05/22/business/2-paths-of-bayer-drug-in-80-s-riskier-one-steered-overseas.html?pagewanted=all.

-Parker-Pope, Tara. Daily Aspirin Is Not for Everyone, Study Suggests, 16 January 2012, http://well.blogs.nytimes.com/2012/01/16/daily-aspirin-is-not-for-everyone-study-suggests/?_r=0.

-Chemical Heritage Foundation. Felix Hoffmann, 11 September 2015, https://www.chemheritage.org/historical-profile/felix-hoffmann.

-Rehab International. Heroin works via its depressant properties, directly impacting the brain upon ingestion, http://rehab-international.org/heroin-addiction/history-of-heroin.

-CBG Network. Heroin Adverts in Spanish Newspapers, 14 November 2011, http://www.cbgnetwork.org/4148.html.

-Askwith, Richard. How aspirin turned hero, 13 September 1998, http://www.opioids.com/heroin/heroinhistory.html.

-Bayer AG, Biographies: Carl Duisberg, http://www.bayer.com/en/carl-duisberg.aspx.

-Inglis-Arkell, Esther. When Opium Was For Newborns And Bayer Sold Heroin, 28 March 2012, The Boston Medical and Surgical Journal, Volume 143

-Prohibiting The Importation of Opium For The Manufacture of Heroin, 3 April 1924, https://babel.hathitrust.org/cgi/pt?id=umn.31951d035475097;view=1up;seq=3.

-Rowley, Matthew. Stoughton's Elixir, an Early Example, 27 March 2010, http://matthew-rowley.blogspot.com/2010/03/stoughtons-elixir-early-example.html.

-Diniejko, Andrzej. The Victorian Web: Addiction. http://www.victorianweb.org/victorian/science/addiction/addiction2.html.

-Journal of the American Medical Association, Volume 53, 1909.

-The Boston Medical and Surgical Journal, Volume 143, 13 December 1900.

-Dr. Rath Foundation. IG Farben and the History of the 'Business With Disease', http://www4.dr-rath-foundation.org/PHARMACEUTICAL_BUSINESS/history_of_the_pharmaceutical_industry.htm

-Narconon. History of Heroin, http://www.narconon.org/drug-information/heroin-history.html.

-Webb, Chris. I.G. Farbenindustrie AG German Industry and the Holocaust, http://www.holocaustresearchproject.org/economics/igfarben.html.

-IG Farben: Official Records from the Nuremberg War Crimes Trials, http://www.profit-over-life.org/.

-United States Holocaust Memorial Museum, Subsequent Nuremberg Proceedings, Case #6, The I.G. Farben Case, https://www.ushmm.org/wlc/en/article.php?ModuleId=10007077.

-CBG Network. Dark Side of Company History ignored, 31 July 2013, http://www.cbgnetwork.org/5200.html.

-FDA. Xarelto (Rivaroxaban) Tablets, May 2016, http://www.fda.gov/Safety/MedWatch/SafetyInformation/ucm367392.htm.

-AHRP. Auschwitz: 60 Year Anniversary – the Role of IG Farben-Bayer, 27 January 2005, http://ahrp.org/auschwitz60-year-anniversary-the-role-of-ig-farben-bayer/.

-Gabbay, Alyssa. Head of Bayer Apologises to Elie Wiesel for Holocaust, 19 December 1995, http://www.apnewsarchive.com/1995/Head-Of-Bayer-Apologises-To-Elie-Wiesel-For-Holocaust/id-7b473229d1d46f012c2639d4648319d7.

-GW World Editorial Staff. Helge H. Wehmeier to be Honored as 2014 Distinguished German-American of the Year, 29 September 2014, http://www.germanworldonline.com/index.php/helge-h-wehmeier-to-be-honored-as-2014-distinguished-german-american-of-the-year/.

Kellogg's

-Narvaez, Darcia. Circumcision: Social, Sexual, Psychological Realities, 18 September 18, 2011, https://www.psychologytoday.com/blog/moral-landscapes/201109/circumcision-social-sexual-psychological-realities.

-Journey Films, John Harvey Kellogg and Adventism Documentary, 2009.

-A&E, Corn Flake Kings: The Kellogg Brothers Biography.

-Soniak, Matt. Corn Flakes Were Invented as Part of an Anti-Masturbation Crusade, 28 December 2012, http://mentalfloss.com/article/32042/corn-flakes-were-invented-part-anti-masturbation-crusade.

-Kellogg, John Harvey. Plain facts for old and young: embracing the natural history and hygiene of organic life, 1887.

-Allen, Carol Easley. Chronology of Major Developments in Adventist Health Promotion & Wellness, 2009, http://archives.adventistreview.org/article/2676/archives/issue-2009-1518/adventist-roots-in-health-promotion/chronology-of-major-developments-in-adventist-health-promotion-wellness

-UT Health Science Center. Dr. John Harvey Kellogg – Inventor of Kellogg's Corn Flakes, 2016, http://library.uthscsa.edu/2014/05/dr-john-harvey-kellogg-inventor-of-kelloggs-corn-flakes/.

-Oneill, Therese. John Harvey Kellogg's Legacy of Cereal, Sociopathy, and Sexual Mutilation, 24 May 2016, http://pictorial.jezebel.com/john-harvey-kelloggs-legacy-of-cereal-sociopathy-and-1777402050.

-Encyclopedia.com. John Harvey Kellogg, 2004, http://www.encyclopedia.com/people/literature-and-arts/asian-and-middle-eastern-art-biographies/john-harvey-kellogg.

-Cereal Project. Kellogg's Krumbles, 2016, http://www.mrbreakfast.com/cereal_detail.asp?id=216.

-Cavendish, Richard. The Battle of the Cornflakes, 2 February 2006, http://www.historytoday.com/richard-cavendish/battle-cornflakes.

-Voll, Michael. 5 Insane Ways Fear of Masturbation Shaped the Modern World, 7 November 2011, http://www.cracked.com/article_19520_5-insane-ways-fear-masturbation-shaped-modern-world.html.

-Galbraith, David. Dr. Kellogg's 15 Most Absurd Medical Contraptions, 26 November 2012, http://gizmodo.com/5963269/dr-kelloggs-15-most-absurd-medical-contraptions/.

-The Urantia Book Historical Society. Dr. John Harvey Kellogg, http://ubhistory.org/storiesandpeople/jhkellogg.html.

-Schwarz, Richard W. John Harvey Kellogg, M.D.: Pioneering Health Reformer, 2006.

Winchester

-Santa Clara County: California's Historic Silicon Valley. Winchester House, https://www.nps.gov/nr/travel/santaclara/win.htm.

-Sulek, Julia Prodis. First full-length biography of rifle heiress Sarah Winchester, by South Bay author Mary Jo Ignoffo, challenges some legends, 5 November 2010, http://www.mercurynews.com/2010/11/05/first-full-length-biography-of-rifle-heiress-sarah-winchester-by-south-bay-author-mary-jo-ignoffo-challenges-some-legends/.

-The History Channel. The History of the Winchester Rifle Documentary.

-InfoPlease. Oliver Fisher Winchester Biography, http://www.infoplease.com/ipa/A0772016.html.

-Van Zwoll, Wayne. Deer Rifles and Cartidges: A Complete Guide to All Hunting Situations, Skyhorse 2012.

-WinchesterGuns.com. Oliver F. Winchester – A man of vision and influence, http://www.winchesterguns.com/news/articles/150-years-of-winchester.html.

-WinchesterGuns.com. Historical Timeline, http://www.winchesterguns.com/news/historical-timeline/historical-timeline-1855-1899.html.

-Winchester Blog. A Man Named Oliver Winchester - From Shirt Maker to Iconic American Figure, 14 March 2016, http://blog.winchester.com/2016/a-man-named-oliver-winchester-from-shirt-maker-to-iconic-american-figure/.

-Patent Yogi. This Day in Patent History – On February 14, 1854 Horace Smith and Daniel Wesson patented the first repeating rifle, 14 February 2016, http://patentyogi.com/american-inventor/this-day-in-patent-history-title-on-february-14-1854-horace-smith-and-daniel-wesson-patented-the-first-repeating-rifle/.

-National Park Service. Battle of the Little Bighorn, https://www.nps.gov/libi/learn/historyculture/battle-of-the-little-bighorn.htm.

-Michno, Greg. Battle of Little Bighorn: Were the Weapons the Deciding Factor, *Wild West Magazine*, June 1998.

Bakelite

-HistoryOfPlastic.com. History of Plastics, http://www.historyofplastic.com/plastic-history/history-of-plastics/.

-USPTO. Patent for First Synthetic Plastic Issued December 7, 1909, 6 December 2001, https://www.uspto.gov/about-us/news-updates/patent-first-synthetic-plastic-issued-december-7-1909.

-Plastics Historical Society. Timeline, http://plastiquarian.com/?page_id=14334.

-Flynn, Tom. Yonkers, Home of the Plastic Age, http://www.yonkershistory.org/bake.html.

-Chemical Heritage Foundation. Leo Hendrik Baekeland, https://www.chemheritage.org/historical-profile/leo-hendrik-baekeland.

-Wirth, Jennifer. Their Bizarre Incestuous Relationship Drove Antony Baekeland To Kill His Heiress Mother, http://allday.com/post/8210-their-bizarre-incestuous-relationship-drove-antony-baekeland-to-kill-his-heiress-mother/.

-SPI. History of Plastics, https://www.plasticsindustry.org/AboutPlastics/content.cfm?ItemNumber=670.

-History.com Staff. This Day In History: 1972 A wealthy heiress is murdered by her son, http://www.history.com/this-day-in-history/a-wealthy-heiress-is-murdered-by-her-son.

-Krajicek, David J. He Will Kill You: Shrink Warned Mother of Baekeland Plastics Heir, 15 June 2015, http://www.nydailynews.com/news/justice-story/kill-shrink-warned-mother-baekeland-plastics-heir-article-1.1114966.

-Schemering, Christopher. The Fall of the House of Baekeland, 15 September 1985, https://www.washingtonpost.com/archive/entertainment/books/1985/09/15/the-fall-of-the-house-of-baekeland/41da760f-dba9-4ac8-bf81-c2469642d657/.

-Barry, Michael Thomas. British Socialite Barbara Baekeland is Murdered - 1972, 17 November 2012, http://www.crimemagazine.com/british-socialite-barbara-baekeland-murdered-1972.

Index